AF348825

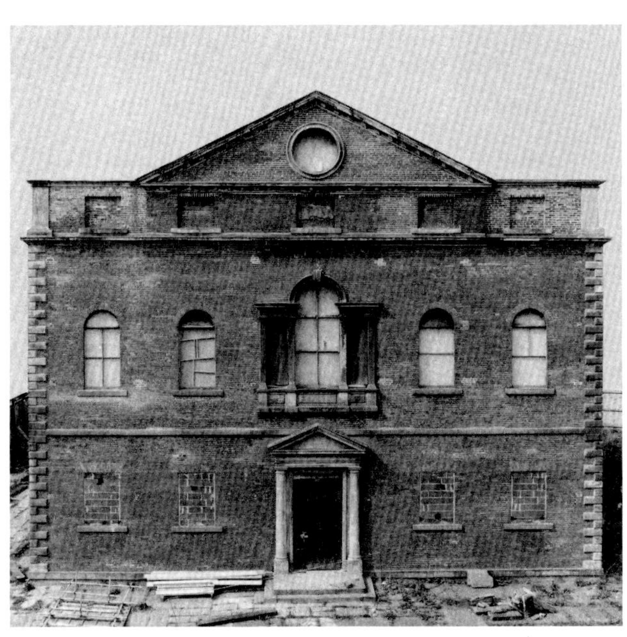

AS ABOVE SO BELOW

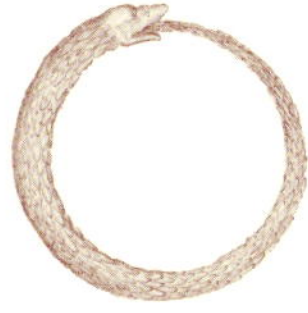

GLEN ONWIN

THE HENRY MOORE SCULPTURE TRUST

1991

FOREWORD

The famous image of Vitruvian Man configuring the square and circle expresses the optimism of the Renaissance in which man was indeed the measure for all things. In a burst of energy that would lead to the Enlightenment and to the scientific discoveries that underpin our present existence, the classically-minded scholars of the Renaissance replaced the mysticism of the Middle Ages with the rationalism of modern man and imposed the concept of 'progress'. In *Form in Gothic*, first published in 1912, Wilhelm Worringer identified mysticism with a tendency towards geometric or abstract art, whereas reason led to a representational art. In both cases, Worringer recognised that the critical element was the relationship of mankind to nature, their separation or integration.

Since the Industrial Revolution our perception of the relationship of mankind to nature is more likely to be expressed in terms of separation than of oneness. In the urbanised late twentieth century Rousseau's noble savage seems as remote as Piers Plowman. And now we have added remorse to our inherited fear of the unpredictable power of nature for good and ill.

Duality and the resolution of opposites — we sometimes speak of a marriage of opposites — gives vitality, but a mindset which opposes nature risks a darker ending.

Square Chapel, Halifax, represents a reasoned response to mysticism expressed physically through geometry. Reason and superstition, science and art, man and nature come together in the work of Glen Onwin.

Onwin's introduction to the building and the development over subsequent months of his ideas into detailed specifications for actual works preceded any apparent interest on his part in its specific history and meaning. Not until the work was fully resolved did he read or discuss this historical background which provides such a resonant context for the further development of the ideas which have made him an artist of steadfast purpose over many years.

The decayed fabric of Square Chapel is not the decrepitude of old age. On the contrary the building still vividly reflects the historical and metaphysical impulses which gave it form and meaning 220 years ago.

We are grateful to the trustees of Square Chapel for enabling us to work in their remarkable building. The resulting installation was exhibited between 8 May and 15 June 1991 as the product of a unique partnership between an artist and a building.

Robert Hopper
Director, The Henry Moore Sculpture Trust

CONTENTS

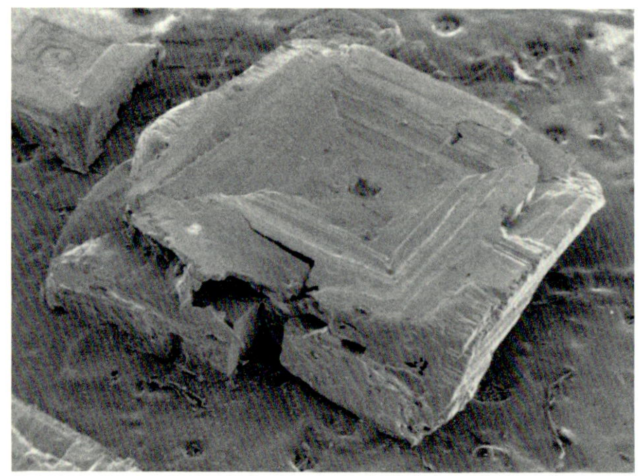

[1]

PERPETUAL POSSIBILITY

Over millennia salt, one of the most ostensibly prosaic substances of common experience, has been invested with not inapposite symbolic significance, given the compound's literal, vital necessity for the sustainment of life. Both oriental and occidental cultures have variously ascribed the mineral with numinous efficacy and in the alchemical pantheon of substances — the arcane practice which putatively sought to successively transmute lesser metals to achieve the perfection of gold, while obscuring a more cogent, involuntary process of psychological insight and spiritual transformation — salt, in conjunction with mercury and sulphur, represented the three universal principles through which a form of conceptual synthesis could be attained. [1]

Fundamental to alchemical thinking was the interrelation and ultimate unity of opposites based on the postulate that all substantive entities were formed from the same basic matter. This underlying idea of oneness, the identity of all things, while alien to mainstream, western systems of belief is in accord with the presuppositions of eastern philosophies such as Tantric Buddhism. The progressive dissolution of the ego and the negation of illusory individuality advanced by Buddhist teaching has a valid correspondence with the inner experience induced by alchemical practices.

Glen Onwin's interest in these and other hermetic beliefs is prompted by an engaged fascination with natural phenomena and the differing ways human beings have related to and apprehended external reality. A preponderant characteristic of his work is the equable value given to all physical entities, animate or inanimate. While certainly eschewing animism, Onwin regards the empathic espousal of nature to be an absolute, intrinsic requirement if incremental, global decline is to be avoided.

An early work *Saltmarsh* (1975) — primarily an empirical exposition of the subtle, physical and botanical cycles of growth and degradation witnessed on a tidal salt-marsh — prefigured certain features to be more clearly discerned in later projects.

The singular environment of a salt-marsh, subject to a continuous, cyclical process of inundation and desiccation, engenders an interplay of inorganic and vegetal growth. In areas of high salinity crystalline development can occur, forming circular saltpans — hostile to organic life — amid expanses of vegetation, while elsewhere plant growth, in binding the tidal silts, actively promotes the generation of new land. [2]

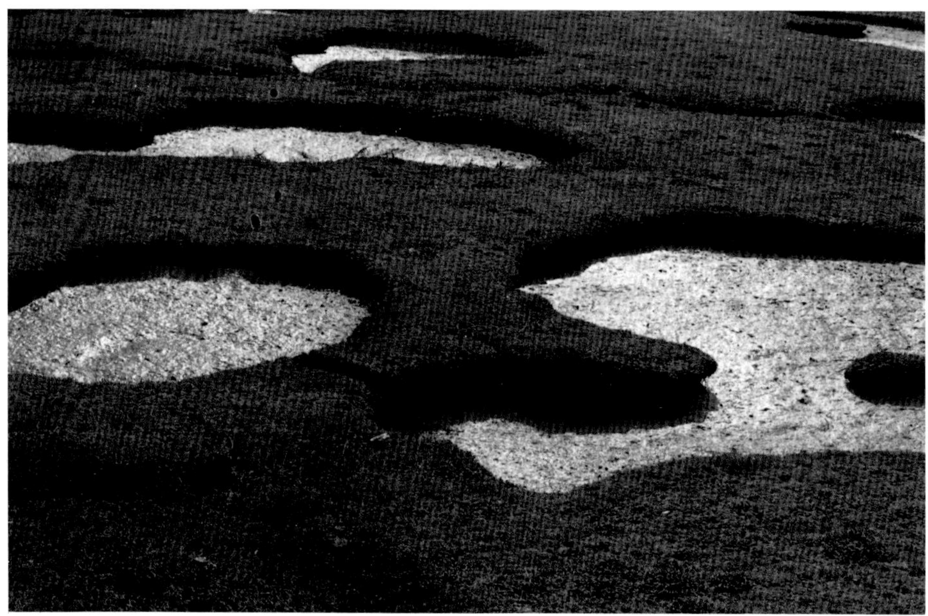

[2]

The rigorous conditions impose a formal coherence on both flora and terrain. Onwin derived from this measure of homogeneity an annular or concentric motif representing, not only the configurations of aqueous incrusion, saline tolerant growth and its disposition, but also the unifying cycle of nature and the harmonious integration of individual parts into a seamless totality. Organic material from the marsh was utilised in the facture of serial studies on substrates of wood or glass exemplifying the characteristic *genius loci*. In order to bond the material to the surfaces Onwin used wax, an archaic medium with rich, cultural associations.

Succeeding the salt-marsh project, *The Recovery of Dissolved Substances* (1978) is an evocation of how humanity has secured salt from seaborne and subterranean sources through processes retaining an almost timeless heritage. Salt's bitter astringency, allied to the long-held belief in the principle of correspondence, led alchemists to attribute to the substance qualities such as blackness and putrefaction, in seeming contradiction to its manifest nature. This psychological aspect, the comprehension of salt as a personification of opposites, is given metaphoric embodiment within the work's structure. The piece proceeds by means of salt-based renderings, photographs, saline trays and evidential artefacts, to impart an experience redolent of the reconstitu-

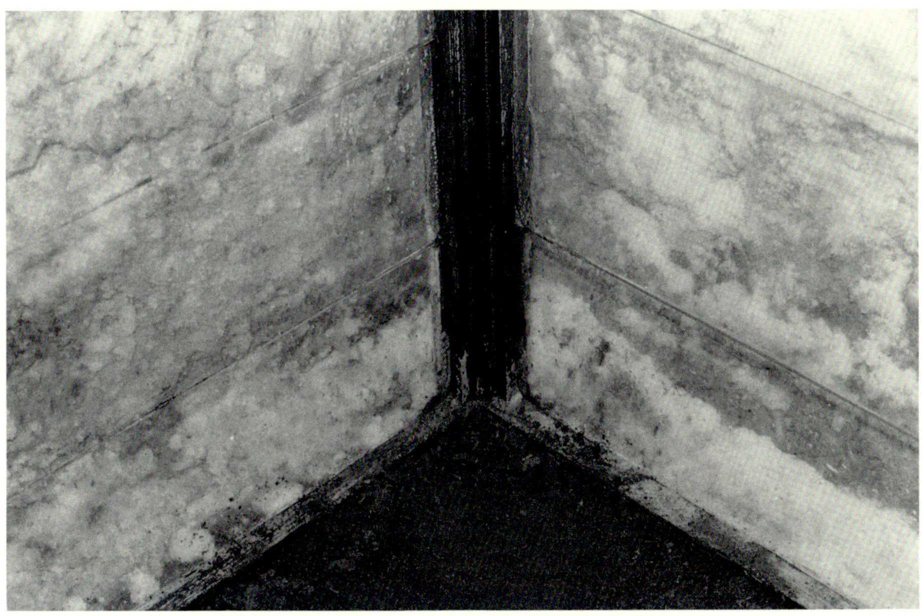

[3]

tion of a history previously denied to verifiable cognition. An antiquarian regard for and absorption in the subject matter, distinguishing the undertaking from more familiar modes of contemporary, rational enquiry, permeates the various elements of the piece.

A second, more enigmatic, component is the intimation of a concealed, underground chamber, created by the artist, the walls of which are lined with a layer of salt retained by glass. The inviolate, cuboid space, its form assimilating that of the salt crystal, is in a continual state of flux due to small changes in ambient humidity. The crystalline particles deliquesce and reform in a cycle which could, hypothetically, continue indefinitely. [3]

In the gallery context the vault has a sparing, almost notional presence: the rudimentary, planar delineation of its parameters; abstracted maquettes; photographic and relief studies of various details. The relative paucity of information, leads the viewer to vivify the space in their imagination, thus facilitating the mind's reflection on the fluid homology of chamber to crystal — macrocosm to microcosm, unhindered by intrusive reality.

The alchemical terminology Onwin employs throughout *Revenges of Nature* (1988) (a major project of 29 individual, though interrelated panels, in preparation for over 5 years) is an indication of his sustained preoccupation

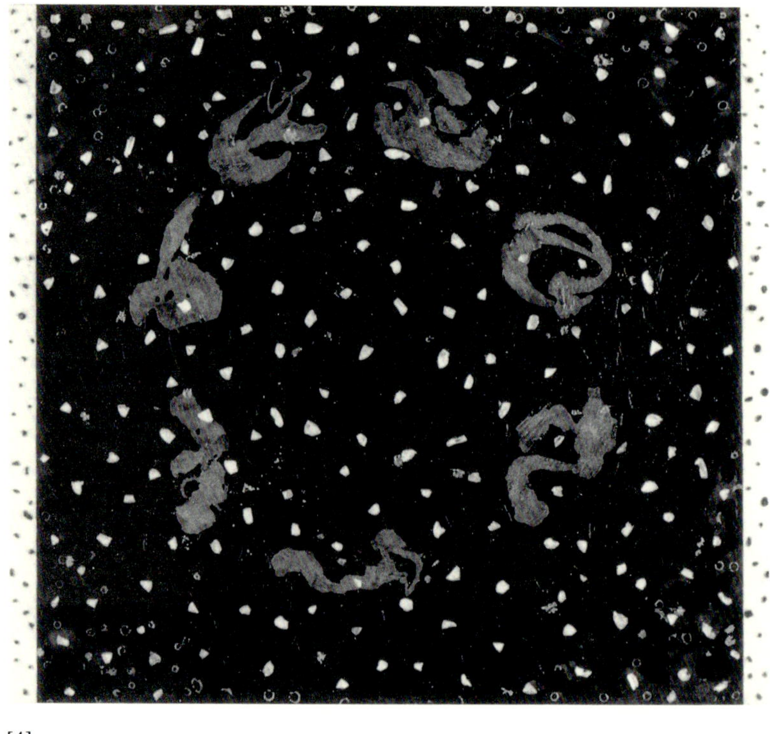

[4]

with the alchemist's art which, while evident in earlier works, tended to operate at a deeper generative level. In this body of work the various stages of the alchemical quest, punctuate the trajectory of the piece and help integrate the relative autonomy of its various aspects.

Revenges of Nature is an account of the Earth's ecological history, albeit partially expressed in the idiom of pre-Enlightenment thought, up to and including human habitation, which instils a salutory admonition of society's current abuse of planetary resources and discloses, in suitably apocalyptic terms, the prospective outcome were current despoilation to continue unabated.

It commences with *Massa Confusa*, at once a representation of primal matter, disseminated in the void prior to the ordering of the cosmos, the pulverised remains of minute, primeval sea-life dispersed in a matrix of carbonaceous rock and the scaled surface of a reptilian creature of geologically, remote origin. The title bears a name associated with the initial stage of

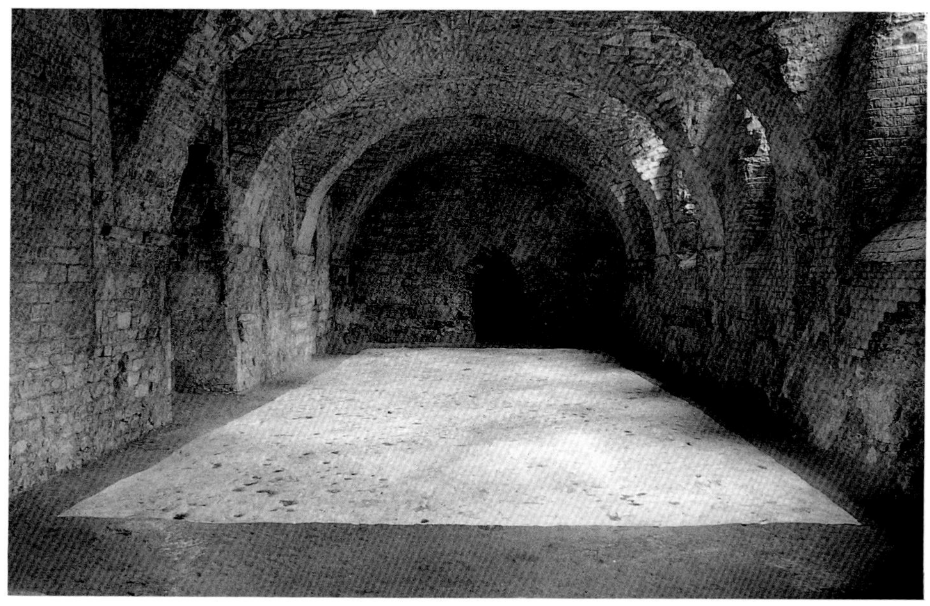

[5]

alchemical operation whereby existing, tainted matter has been reduced to a basic uniformity before the procedure of regeneration could begin.

The simultaneous depiction of imaginary and historic episodes typifies the compound intent borne by many of the works in the series. Individual pieces of essentially documental import are, via contextual influence, conferred with ubiquitous relevance. The cyclical leitmotiv of earlier projects aptly summarises the unfolding of *Revenges of Nature* as the later works prognosticate a sterile, moribund world ending in disintegration and dispersal. The tenebrous tone is somewhat mitigated by its concluding work, *Vortex of Degradation*. Approximating the form of a mandala described in an illimitable extensity and comprised of marine and other natural fragments, it transcends the contingency of experience to engage with the vast, ineluctable continuum of space and time. [4]

Of Nature's Obvious Laws and Processes in Vegetation (1990) was a temporary installation created in the undercroft of the Bishop's Palace adjacent to

Lincoln Cathedral. The vaulted, stone room, dating from the twelfth century, measures fifty by twenty-five feet and is lit transversely by a series of windows located high on the east-facing wall.

Onwin elected to prime the beaten, earth floor with a thin layer of molten wax which solidified to form a pale, opalescent membrane echoing the contours of the uneven ground beneath. In numerous, shallow cavities dispersed over the surface — the result of aerial precipitation — he seeded the wax with chemical solutions and plant extracts which, over a period of weeks, would exhibit patterns of simple growth. The resulting miscellany of organic and inorganic proliferation suggested an emblematic reconciliation of the oppositional dualism science imposes on the natural world. [5]

The installation was entitled after a manuscript by the great, seventeenth century theorist, Isaac Newton who was a noted devotee of alchemical lore. In this, Newton treats the distinction between 'vulgar chymistry', the imitation of mechanical changes in nature, and 'a more subtile secret & noble way of working' which referred to the belief, that obtained during his time, of an animating agent or spirit inherent in all mineral and vegetable matter which he sought to harness through experimentation. Newton regarded gaining access to the sacred, operative actions of nature to be a supreme accomplishment entailing profound, moral responsibilities. Onwin's piece pays discreet homage to the prescience of Newton's protective reverence for nature, an issue which is now of such crucial, world-wide importance. For almost two decades his own work has perceptively conveyed this obligation and has eloquently confronted the need for a complete transvaluation of humanity's, hitherto, predatory relationship with the natural environment.

James Birrell

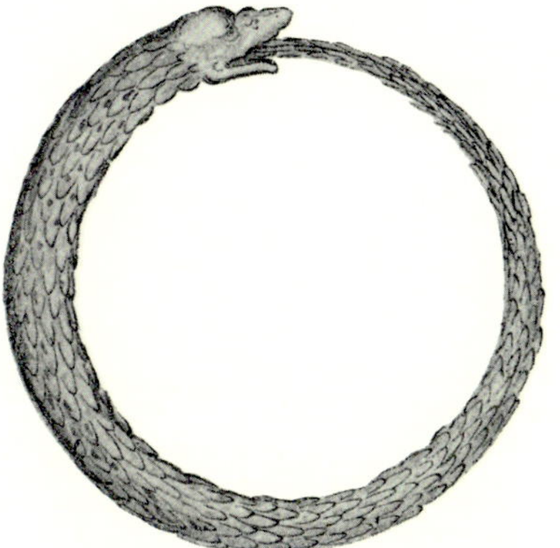

H He Li Be B C N O F Ne Na Mg
Al Si P S Cl Ar K Ca Sc Ti V Cr
Mn Fe Co Ni Cu Zn Ga Ge As Se
Br Kr Rb Sr Y Zr Nb Mo Tc Ru
Rh Pd Ag Cd In Sn Sb Te I Xe Cs
Ba La Ce Pr Nd Pm Sm Eu Gd Tb
Dy Ho Er Tm Yb Lu Hf Ta W Re
Os Ir Pt Au Hg Tl Pb Bi Po At Rn
Fr Ra Ac Th Pa U Np Pu Am Cm
Bk Cf Es Fm Md No Lr Unq Unp

PROJECTED THOUGHTS ON
SQUARE CHAPEL, HALIFAX

A Note — 16.2.91

From a door where no door should be,
entering the light upper space
a square room, a square tank
twenty paces by twenty paces,
islands of black wax on black liquid,
slow continuous evaporation the formation of cubic salt crystals,
white on black,
Nigredo
laid to waste, chaos,
disrupted image.
Through a matrix of timber joists the plywood roof exposed,
a central damaged ring
the first uroboros,
reflected.
Arches, partial circles, grey low walls, liquid stillness,
the dull sounds from the street.
Reflection.
Columns of white, square columns, columns with capitals,
fragments of past decoration.
Flaking paint, crosshatched mortar keyed for plaster,
concrete floor, dust,
newness.
Four windows on the entrance wall, five on the wall opposite,
five to the left, five to the right,
the most preserved in front still with glass,
now broken.

Plasterwork intact, on terra-cotta on terra-verte.
From the light
the descent;
a new bannister, a landing, then more steps down
into darkness from the light
past very broken walls and panels of electric fuse boxes,
a complex of rooms, doors and sealed windows,
cold moist air,
a flagstone floor.
A long passageway;
the glow of ambient light,
a glass column of green,

Pharmacy
dual liquid pillars of red and green
and to the right,

Its Nurse is the Earth
bituminous surface, illuminated floor, vials of vegetal matter,
coarse blue green crystal growth, cupric sulphate,
sodium chloride, tar.
Darkness around.
Metal edged pitch lustre, dimly lit but reflecting on walls
revealing brass, copper, steel,
engraved squares with illegible significance,
they are the signatures of the elements
one hundred and five perhaps more.
Moving then looking into.

The One to The One
a double square of liquid,
black liquid, white liquid, black white, white black
opposites.
Green lit water reflecting on ceiling,
peeling paint, cement rendered walls, terra-cotta brick.

Black brine with inorganic saline residue,
gypsum, sea water deposit, white stone.
White brine with organic black,
compressed,
the green plants from the carboniferous era.
Two hundred and forty million years,
black lump coal in milky liquid
encrusted salt a concentrated brine evaporite,
polarity,
the work of the sun.
To the right

Uroboros

immaculate square illuminated green,
the strong circle of the transparent coil running continuously
around and around
girding the earth.
Salt laden, clear and green water
reflecting in aluminium the dense internal ring
central to the room.
Below
liquid light mirrored
above
a near square projecting its own serpent image
the vaguely discernable circle.
Green liquid column, red liquid column;
leaving the green
the ascent
to the black square and the optical pink of daylight.

'That which is above is like that which is below
and that which is below is like that which is above,
to accomplish the miracles of the one thing.'

NIGREDO

Laid to Waste

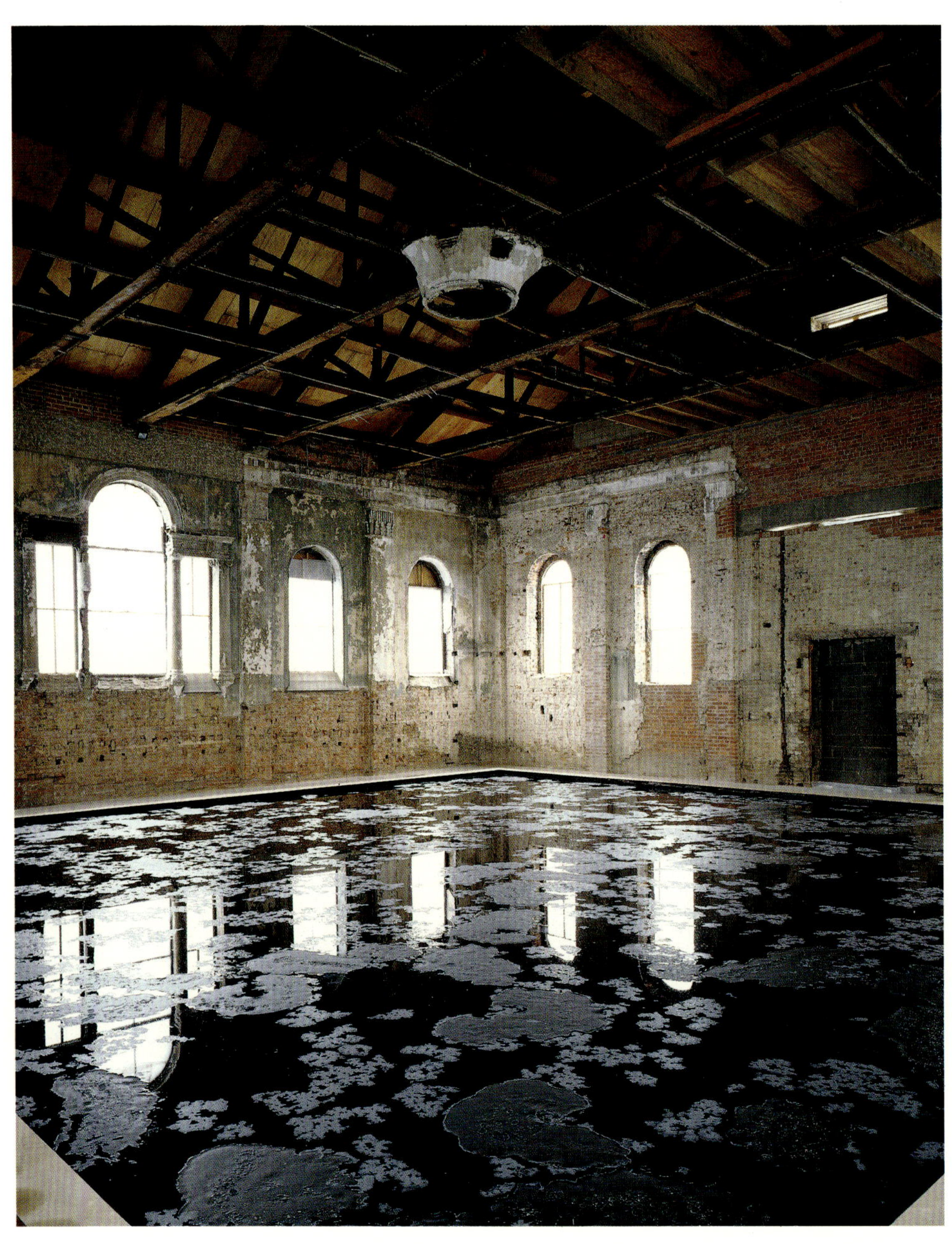

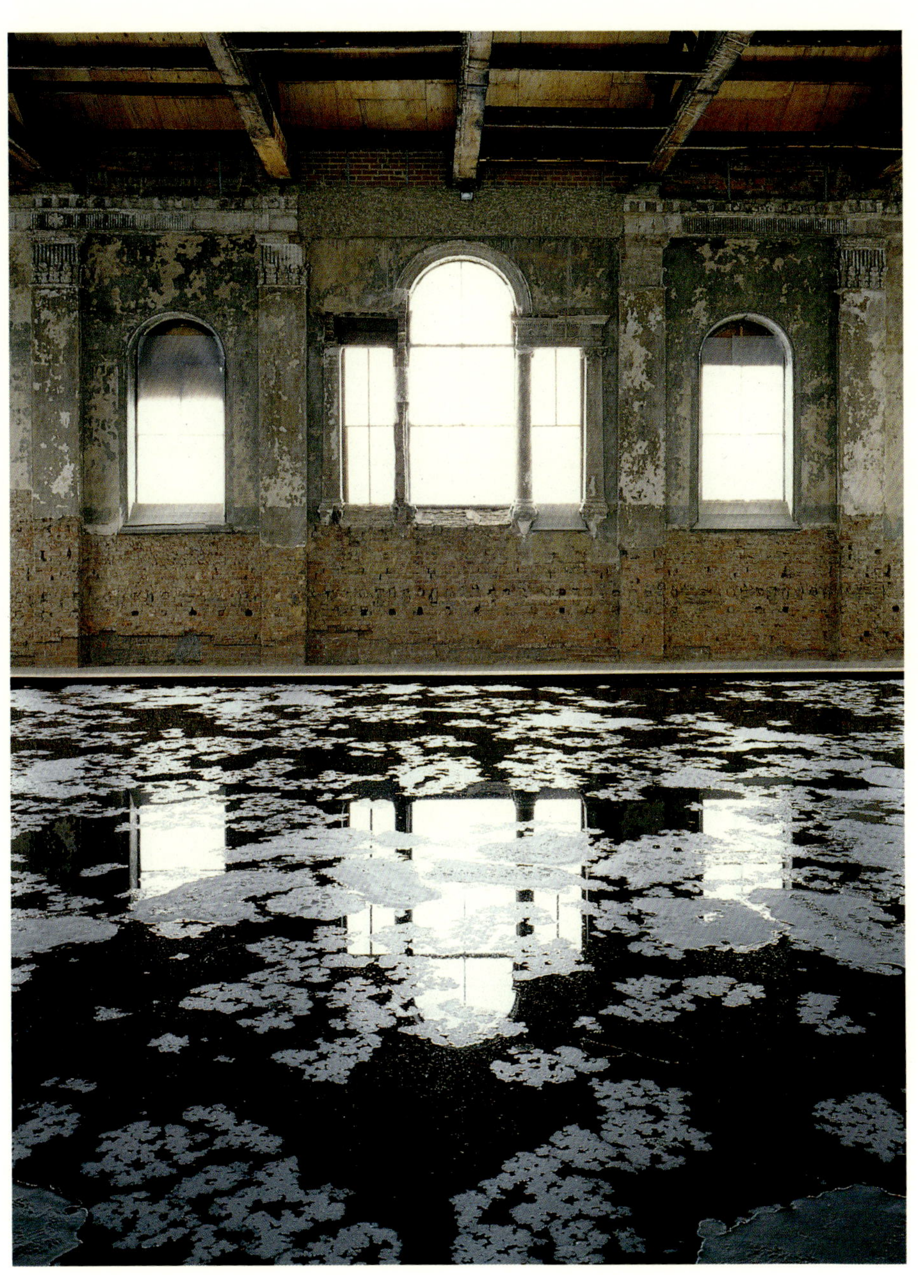

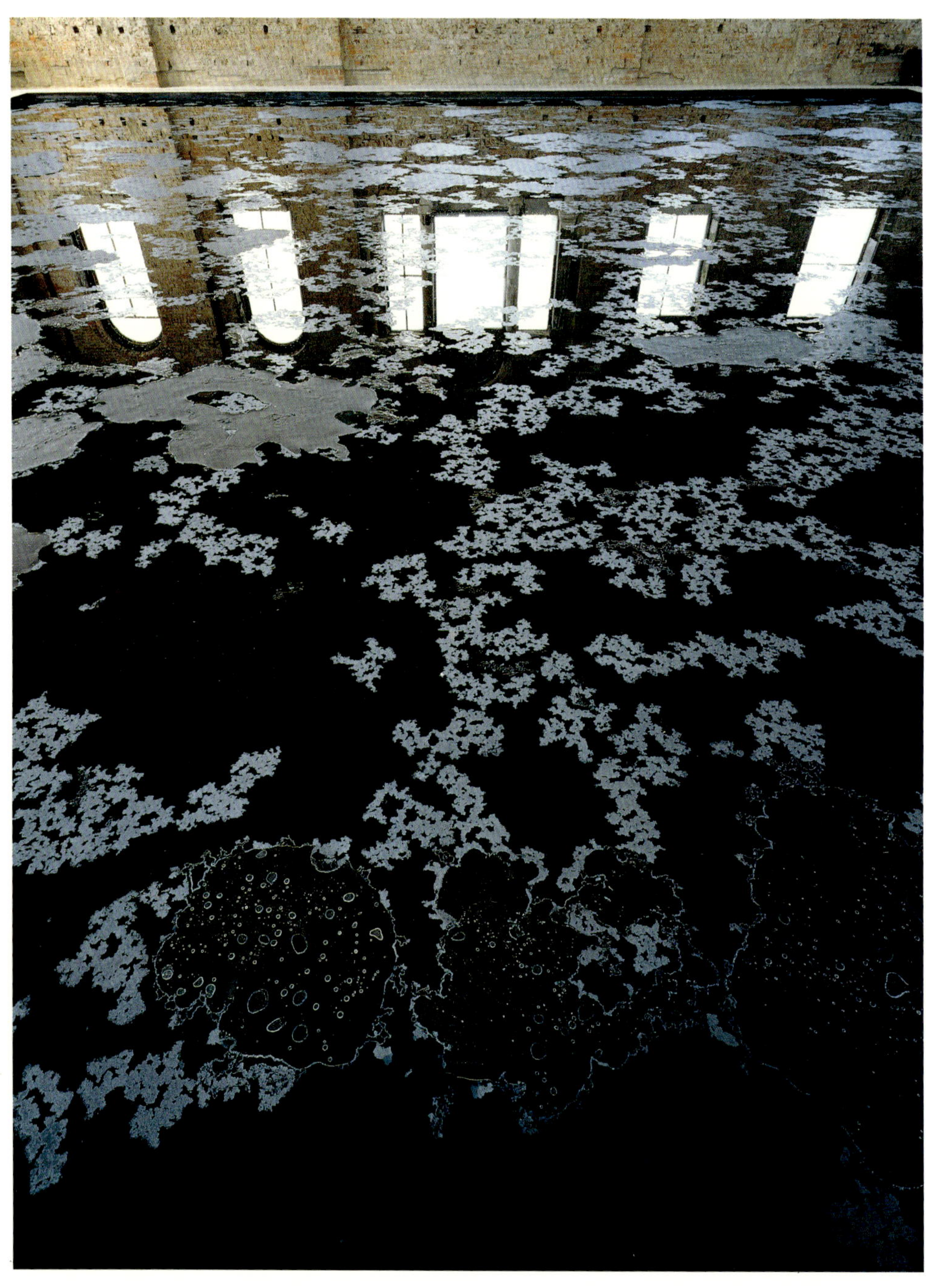

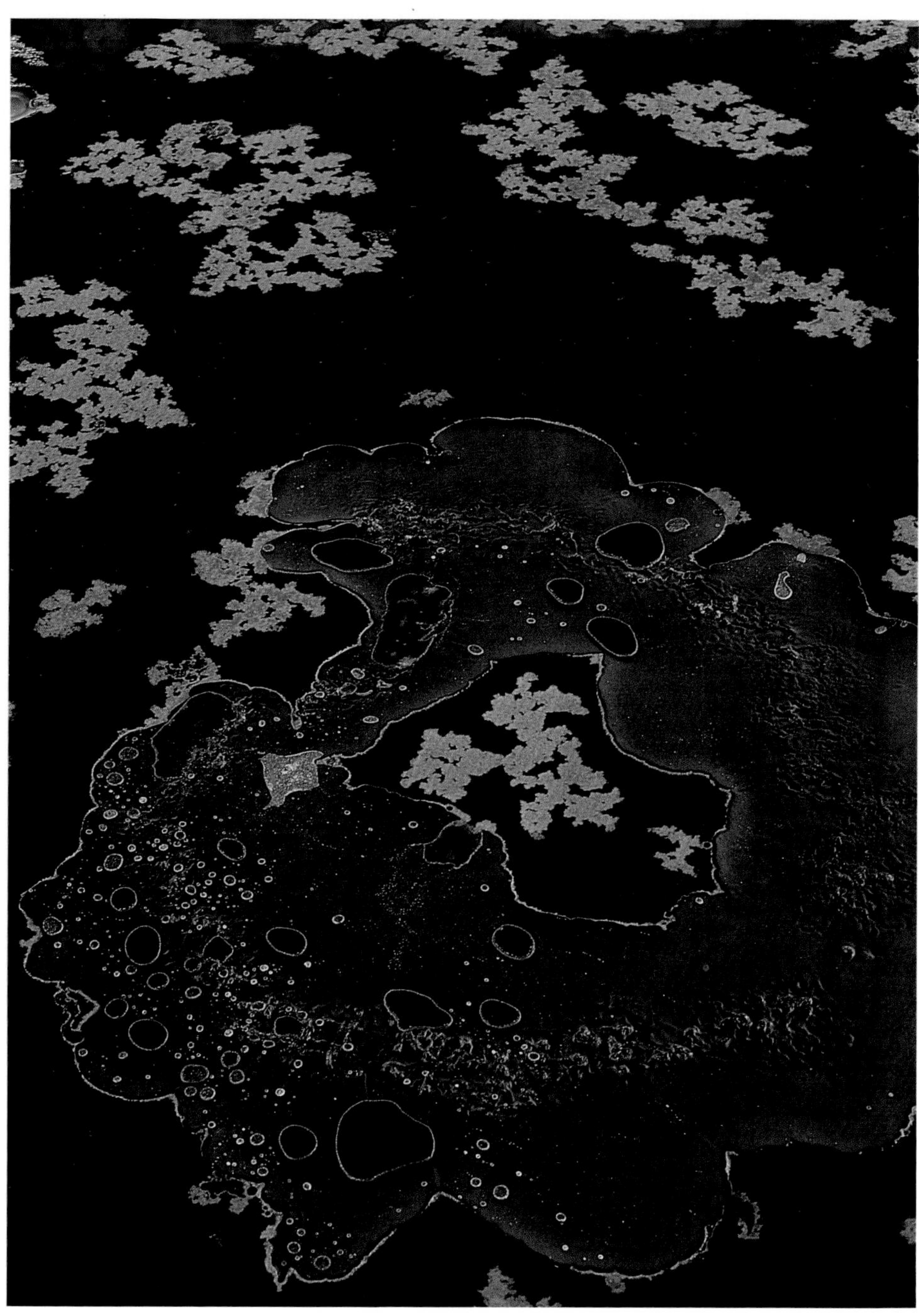

PHARMACY

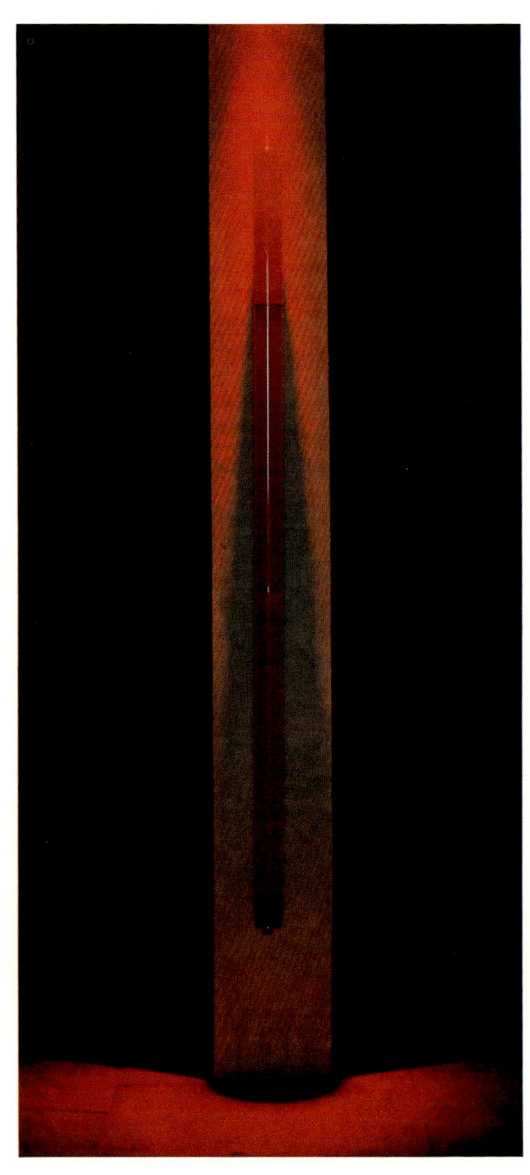

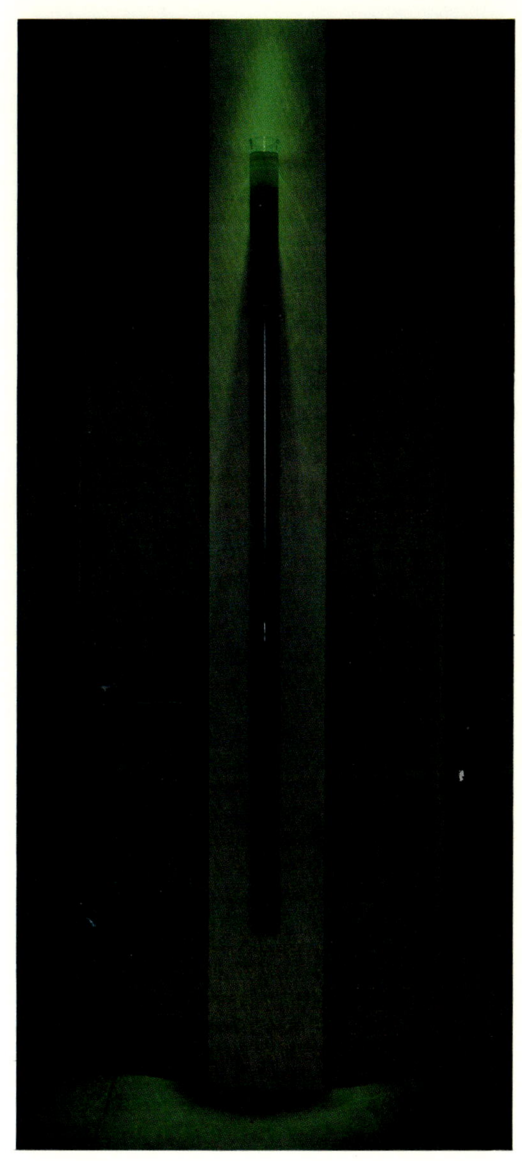

ITS NURSE IS THE EARTH

Carbon

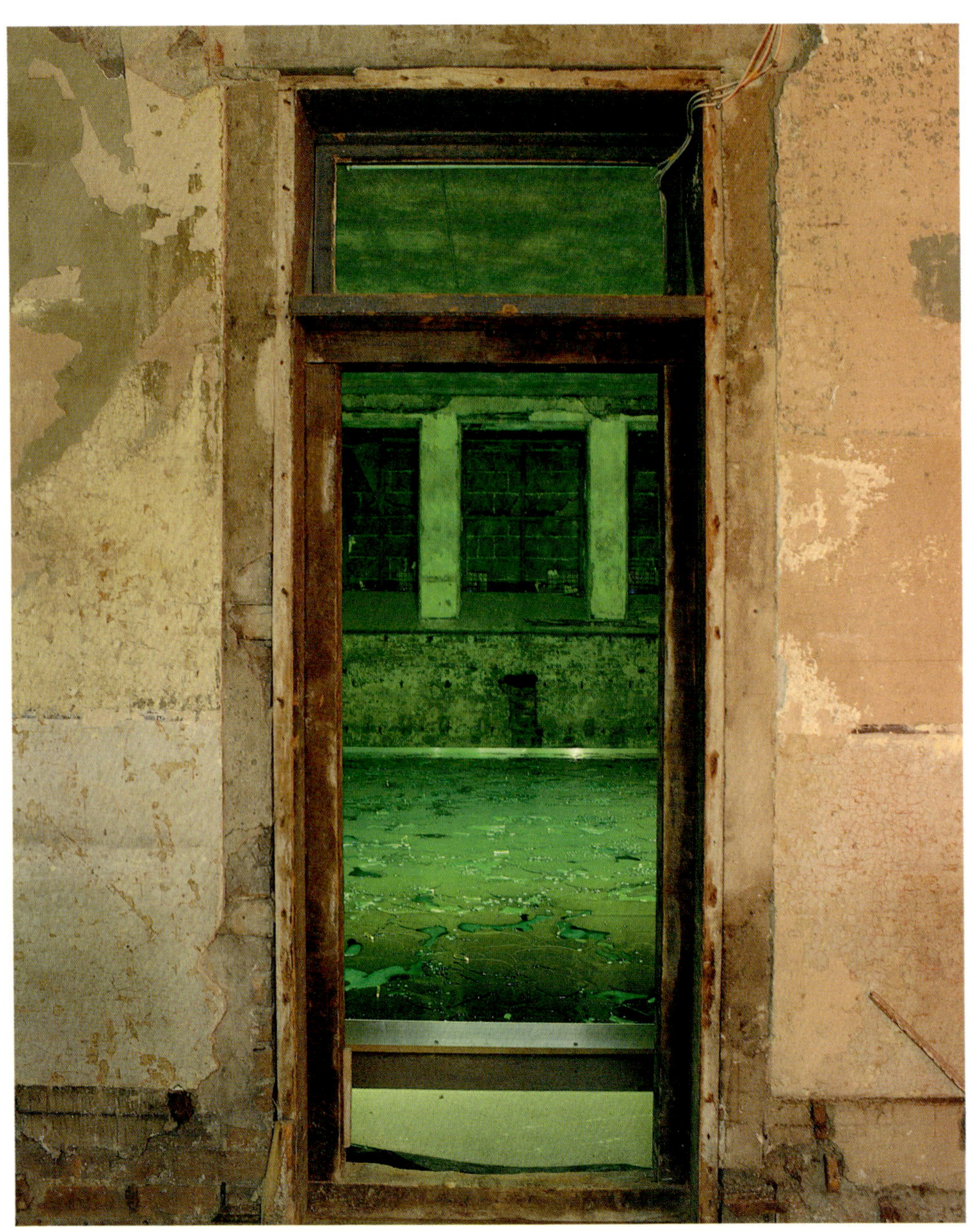

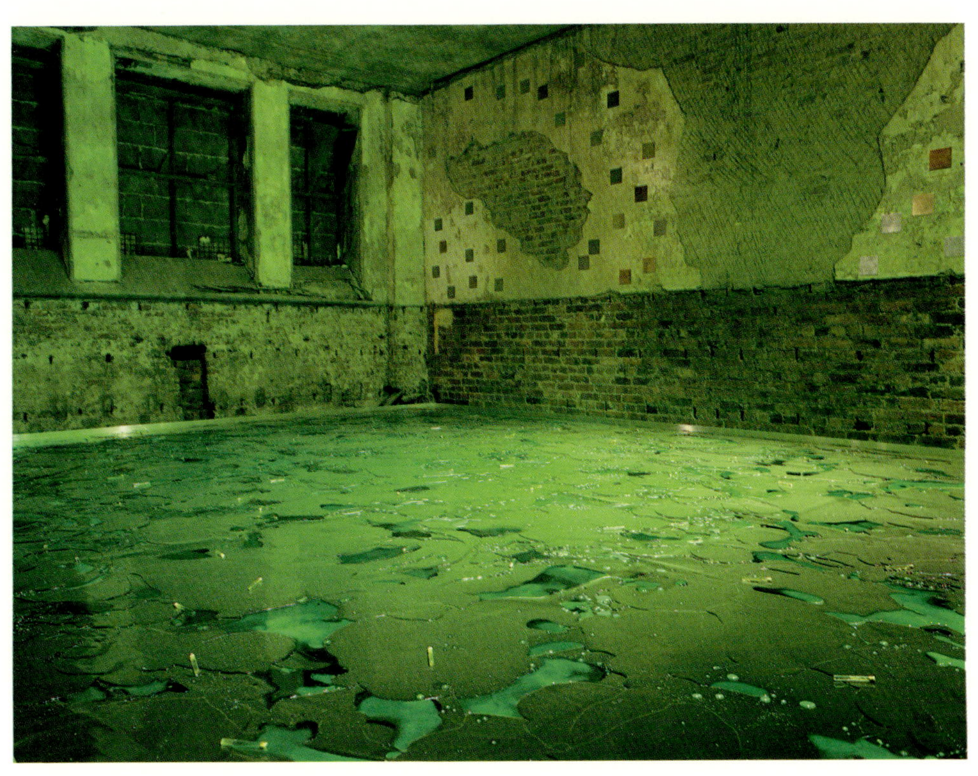

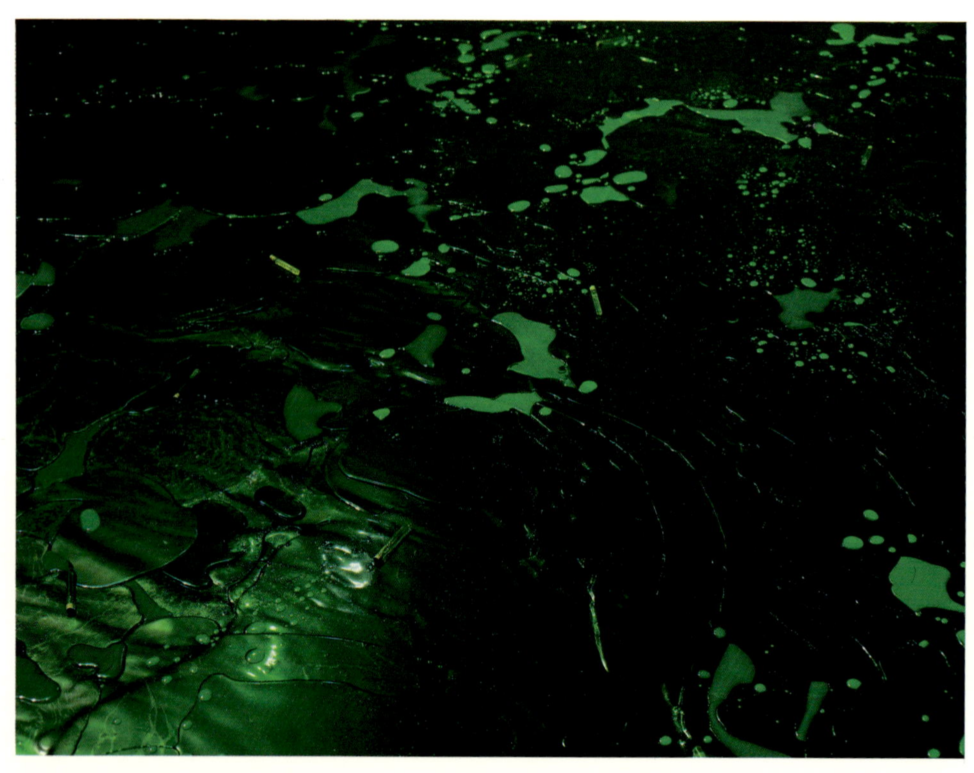

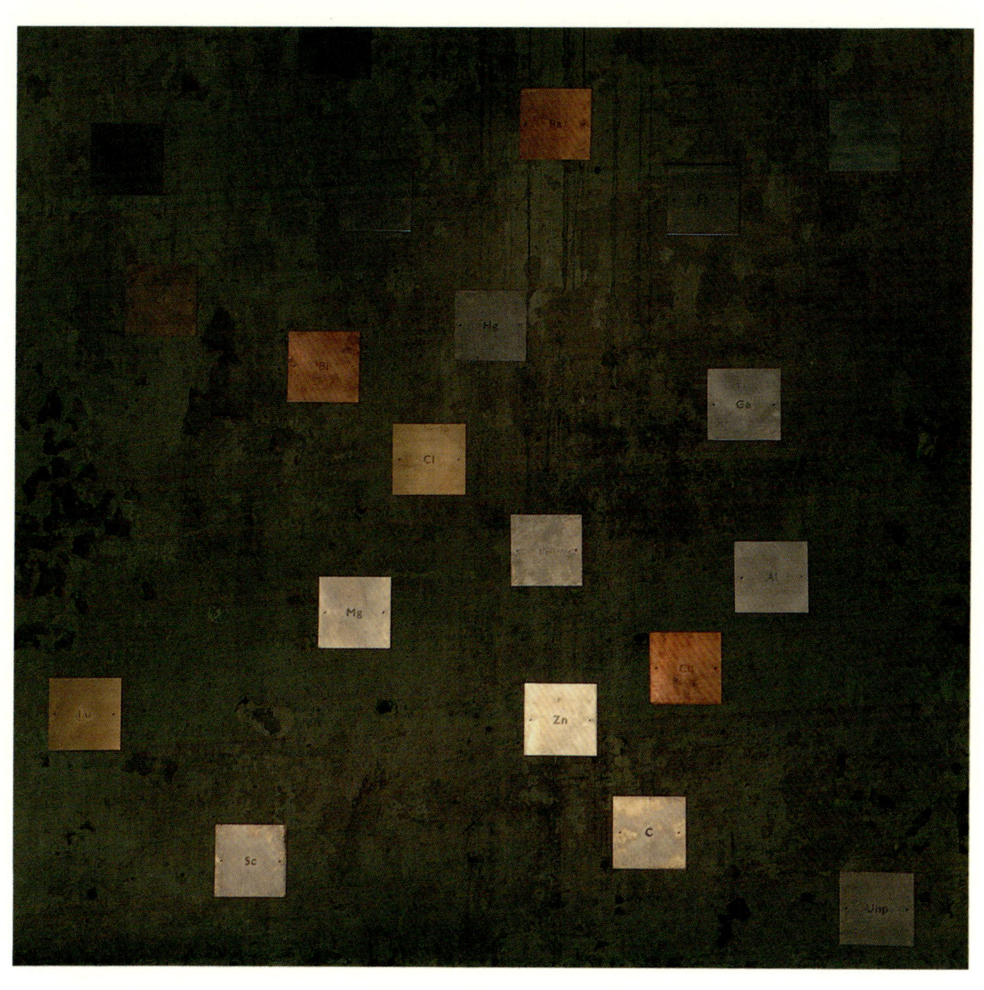

Hg
Ge
Bi
Cl
Mg
Al
Cu
Zn
Au
Sc
C
Unp

THE ONE TO THE ONE

Organic / Inorganic

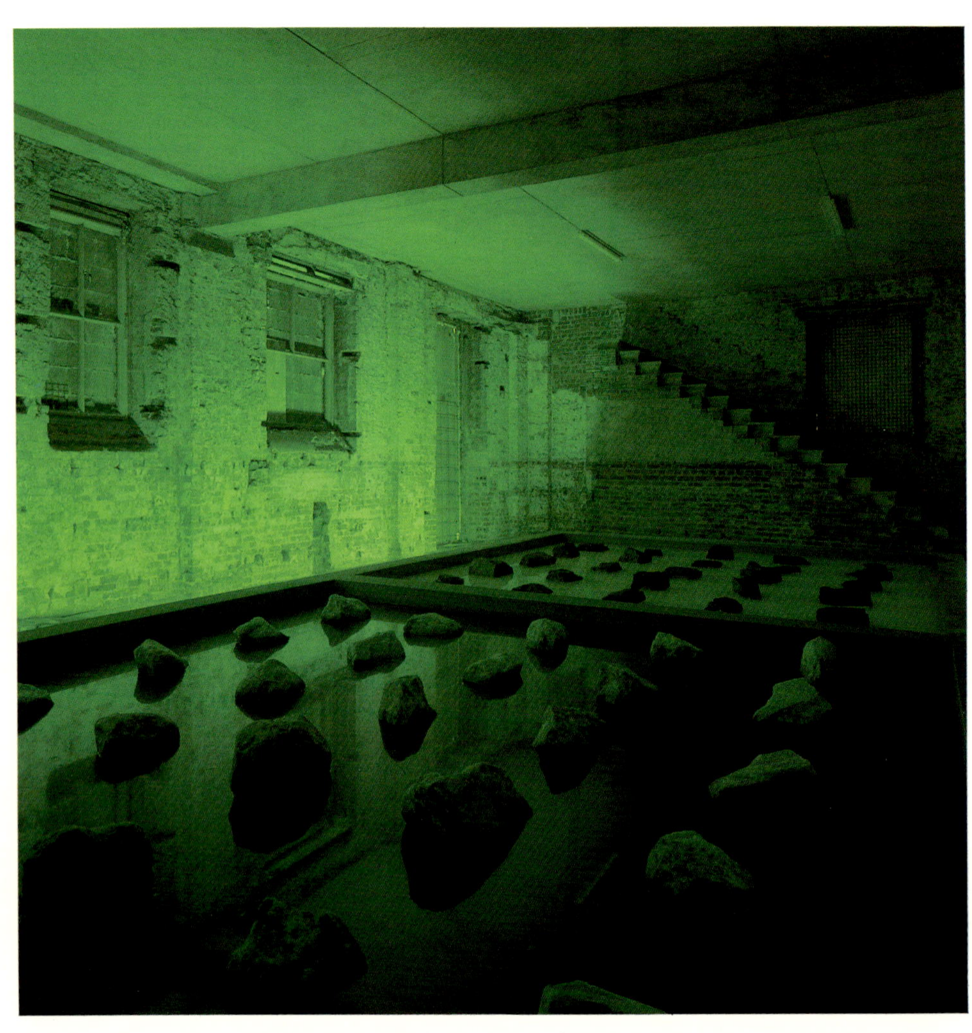

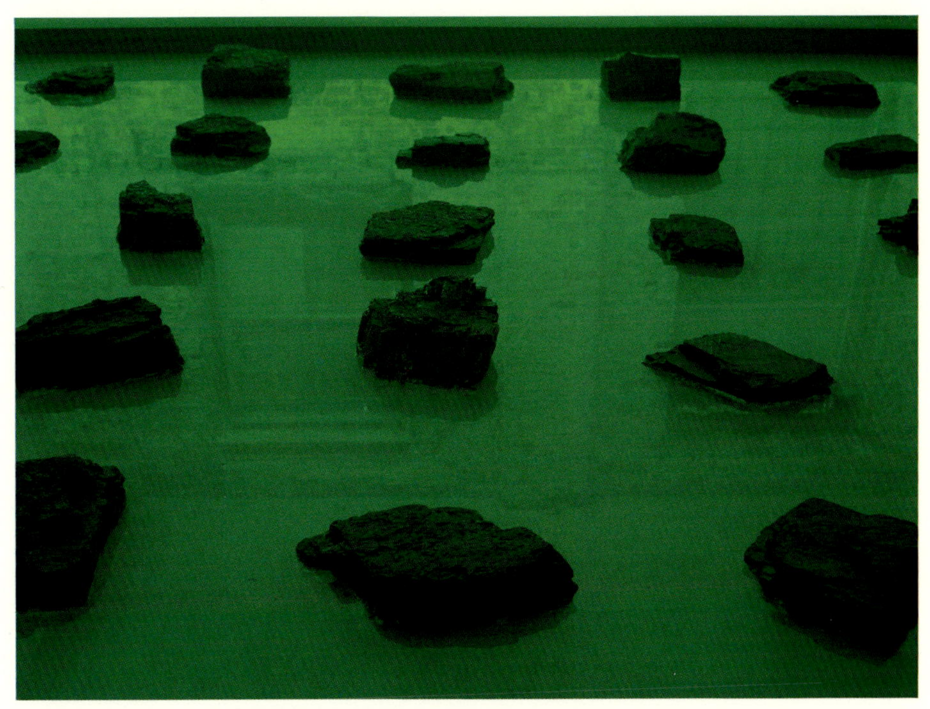

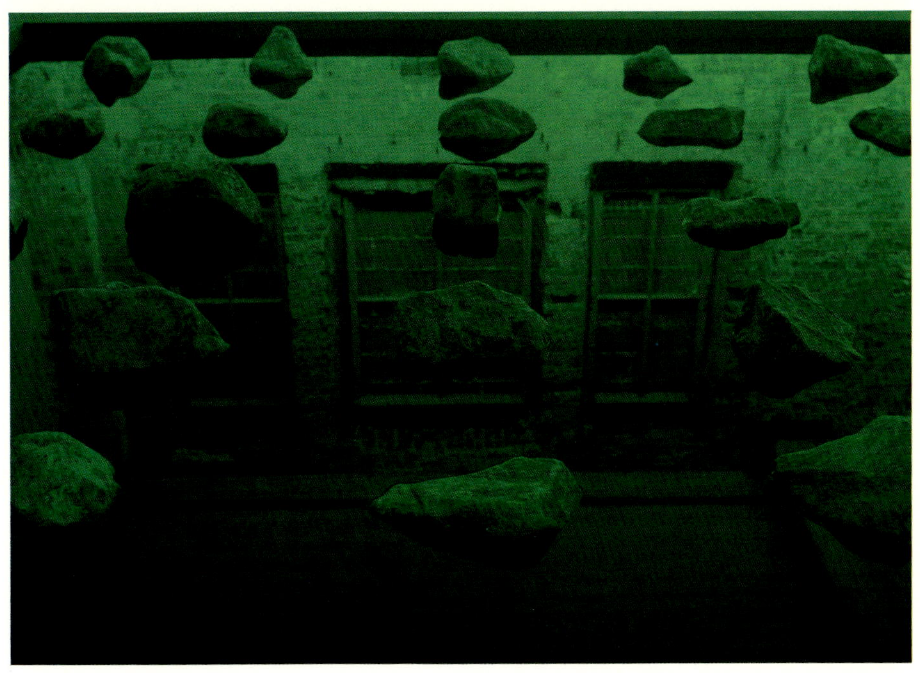

UROBOROS

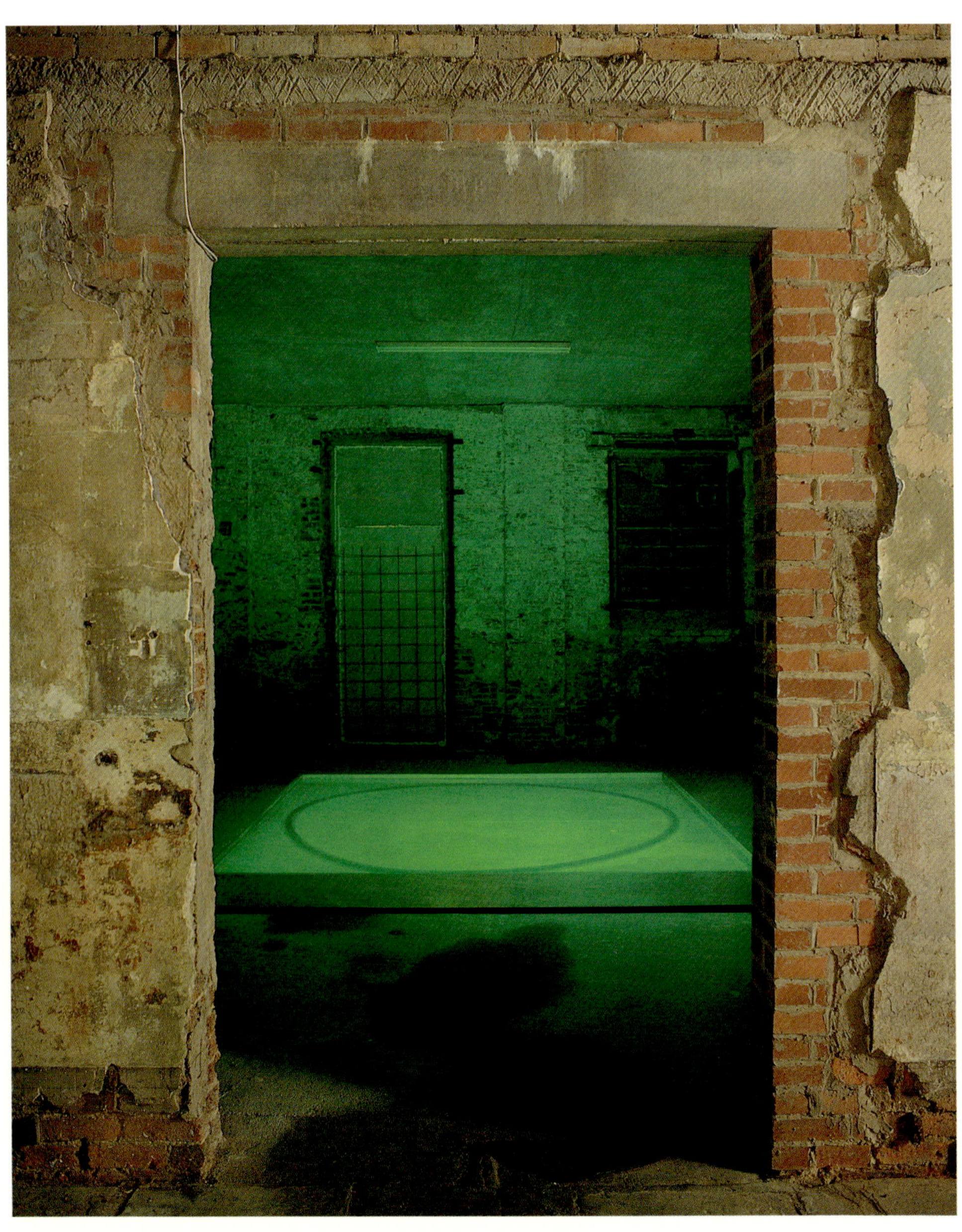

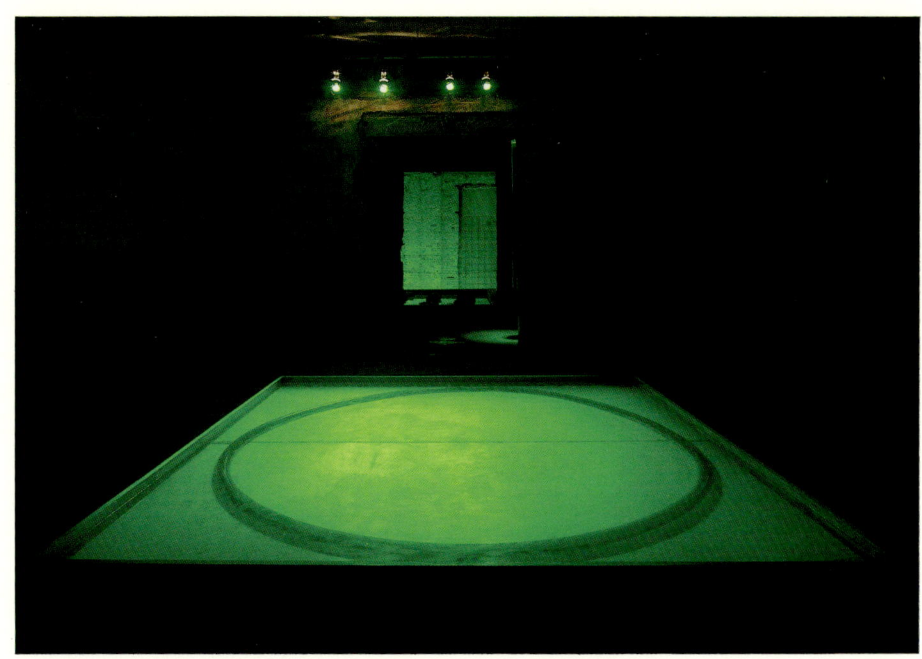

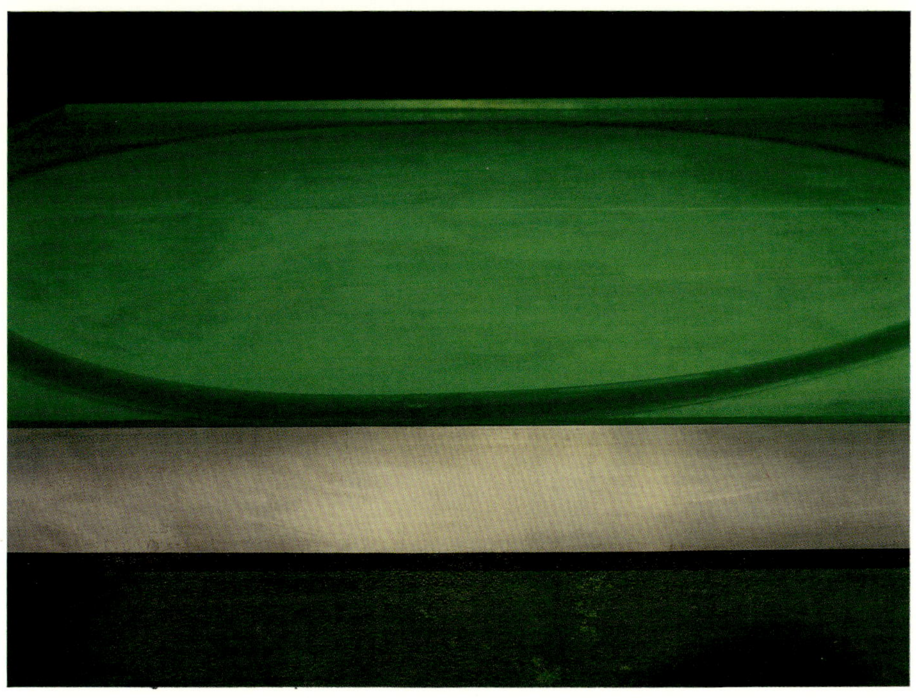

THE ABOVE LIKE THE BELOW

They say that artists find their themes. In Glen Onwin's case the theme found *him*; a single event inspired a project with its own internal consistency, capacity for extrapolation and potential for unifying disparate areas of concern. Analysis of three stages of his extended meditation — a book which sets out its premises, a set of paintings, and his Square Chapel installation — may help to introduce this twenty-year train of thought.

Onwin's formative period coincided with the rise of Conceptual art and the reaction against it. Every Conceptualist had previously been a Minimalist, one critic announced, as if a straight line led from one to the other.[1] If only things had been that simple. From 1965 to 1967 important debates about art and materiality had been triggered by Minimalist artworks and manifestos. Non-anthropomorphic, anti-transcendental, Minimalist sculpture revised prevailing vocabulary, as 'sculpture' became 'object' and 'space' became 'place'. Critics still argue about whether the result was primarily conceptual or phenomenological in effect.[2] The assumption of a direct route to Conceptual art was all too easy, then: the product of Modernist 'progress' viewed as an endless series of reductions. In fact, the last years of the 60s showed a simultaneous swing in opposite directions: towards language on the one hand and physicality on the other. Suddenly, it seemed, attention was focused on materials, almost for their own sake.

In Europe a form of conceptualism had existed since the time of Yves Klein and Piero Manzoni. Despite this, the greatest artist of the postwar period never abandoned his preoccupation with the object nature of art. Joseph Beuys's approach could be described as allotropy. Consider his use of fat. Fat triangles could be made to fill the corners of rooms. Fat could be moulded, as when he used it to fill a redundant area in a pedestrian underpass, then displayed the result. His *Fettstuhl* became a potent political icon during the time of his sacking from the Düsseldorf academy. But it was the literal, not the metaphorical versatility of fat that appealed to him most. It could harden, as in the underpass piece. It could soften: a film shows the artist sinking his buttocks into solidified fat. It could become liquid; in his fictional *curriculum vitae* he claimed to have exhibited bubbling pans of it in 1963.[3] It even possessed lifesaving powers: fat, he claimed in his own, apparently unverifiable version of his early life, had been among the substances applied to his wounded, frostbitten body when it was discovered by passing Tartars after his fighter plane crashed in the Urals.[4]

Beuys's predilection for materials which existed in a range of modalities, an approach that could be termed 'material allotropy', suited the late 60s situation, in which a tension between idea and solidity was felt. 'Post-Minimalism', one term to describe the prevailing trend, had to be made to embrace mathematically based experiment, for example, as well as body-related activities. One major artist, at least, moved between these extremes. Robert Smithson practised a *conceptual* allotropy. His *Spiral Jetty* existed in the form of drawings, an essay, a film and a large-scale outdoor sculpture [1]. In addition, it served as a springboard for future projects: a museum of the *Spiral Jetty* was planned, with a cinema showing the *Spiral Jetty* film.

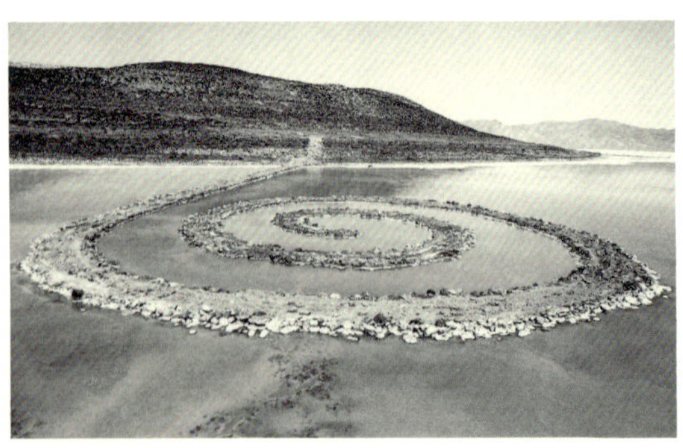

[1]

Smithson's work wavered between the fictive and the all-too-real, giving his entire output a self-generating polyvalence. For example, film could never interpret the *Spiral Jetty*, photography was unable to encompass it, and when it was inundated it existed as no more than a memory. Smithson geared his work to encompass this gamut of separate but related existences. By nature, he aimed too high and his work lapsed into melancholy and intellectual clowning. A friend remembered the day he came across the word 'disappointment' in a thesaurus. 'I love it, I love it, I love it,' he yelled.

The discussion point of late 60s art could be reduced to a single proposition. If materiality — and, not incidentally, materialism — was to be redefined and the work of art was no longer to assume the form of an object, what then would art look like and mean? One way of coping with the question was to avoid simplistic dichotomies by the use of 'allotropic' methods. The idea of a graduated scale linking 'object' and 'concept', of settling at points on this scale and offsetting them in order to acknowledge the problematic nature of the exercise, was a realistic way of solving a complex problem or of suggesting a third term, an absent subject, changed as — modern scientists have taught us — every 'thing' is changed, by observation. Walking along the coast near Dunbar one Sunday afternoon, Glen Onwin happened to find what seemed to be a flooded field. 'I suddenly realised that the water was actually rising,' he told an interviewer. 'When I explored it further I realised it was a salt marsh . . . Every single part was like every other part. Everything was part of a process — the muddy water drawn into the field, the deadening effect of the salt, the salt which also sustained life.'[5] Neither space in the abstract nor any specific object had attracted his attention, but a site which stimulated thoughts and emotions. It was the beginning of a sequence of work which has continued for twenty years. Obviously, the choice of the salt marsh represents a solution to the unworkable 'object versus concept' mentality of the period. Like Minimalist sculpture, parodied later in the photographs of assembled saltblocks, every part resembled every other part and seemed to belong to the world, not the gallery. And the cycle of water rising, of the constant dissolution and sublimation of the salt, ran the gamut from invisibility to visibility and back.

Onwin's encounter eventually led to his book *The Recovery of Dissolved Substances*[6] with five sections which compare one method of obtaining salt with another: from sun-dried salt on dark earth to the outdated salt works and its single employee, practising a profession which had scarcely changed since the Middle Ages. In 'Coastland', the first section, fictitious archaic salt-working tools were shown alongside images with horizons which recall that point of crystallisation when liquid becomes solid and a past tense is summoned, before what is dissipated re-forms and is used. After 'Elementary Chemistry', with photographs of wooden troughs half immersed in water, the stagnant beginnings of a change of state at 'the edge of a system where salt meets earth', the third contains the book's only pictured person, Cyril Hitchens, an employee at the Red Lion Saltworks near Nantwich, ladling salt from steaming vats and tipping it into containers where it will harden and be stored. From pictures of these equal-sized, geometrically-shaped slabs onwards, the book takes an increasingly abstract turn. A cubic, subterranean chamber is shown, with walls on which salt has crystallised and been covered with glass. Its air of decay is reinforced by the fact that the room remains secret and exists solely in photographs, to be 'experienced only in the imagination'. And a final section contains images of bubbling, cracking and crystallisation.

Half material, half artificial, salt is presented as subject to a drama of loss and restoration. What Onwin describes as 'the recovery of the real and a sense of past reality' takes place in atmospheres of putrescence or stagnation, in secret places with a single, lonely craftsman who belongs in the deep past. If, as ancient cultures claimed, memory is the mother of poetry, then the 'recovery' which is the artist's chosen theme can be translated as the act of artistic creation itself, an act in which the insubstantial assumes a more tangible form. Hence, perhaps, the combination of natural *and* unnatural conditions. Nurtured by silence, fed by underground waters which seem to well up from the darkness and loneliness of subterranean chambers, the process of crystallisation of salt, solid from liquid, resembles Romantic metaphors for inspiration. And, like a Romantic wanderer, the artist is drawn to an *omphalos* or sacred site, a point where power is fixed and concentrated.[7] As Onwin is at pains to point out, this is a place of margins, a strait not only between land and sea but also between states of being, a site which attracts him for reasons he does not understand.

Boundaries stop the traveller in his tracks, putting him in a state which resembles that of a threshold. In this case the geographical setting offered a parallel to the artist's own state of mind. It triggered deep responses: of the womb, of baptism, of the sea, and, since scientists tell us that the internal salinity levels of whales, mice and humans are exactly the same, of community.[8] For Onwin, reaching a new stage of artistic maturity, it meant experiencing a new sense of responsibility and belonging. For him the saltmarsh experience was a *rite de passage*. In Jungian terms, it relates to the process of 'centroversion', described as 'the innate tendency of a whole to create unity within its parts and to synthesise their difference in unified systems'.[9] Since centroversion controls the compensatory processes which preserve the unity of the whole, that whole becomes a 'self-creating, expanding system' — in other words, a system resembling a saltmarsh.[10] Yet something was missing. By the end of the saltmarsh experience, reported much later in the *Recovery...* book, 'conjunction' — the title of the final section — has still to take place. Unity is possible, even imminent, but has yet to be attained; 'separation before joining' are the last words of the text. In psychoanalytic terms, 'conjunction' involves death and rebirth, transformation and loss, in fact the losses and gains of the psychoanalytic process itself, which Jung observed, was the only 'initiation process' practised in the West today. In its Latin form *coniunctio*, it is borrowed, like so much of Jung, from the language of alchemy.

At the heart of Christianity lies a myth of transsubstantiation. Central to alchemy was a parallel myth of converting base metals to gold. For many centuries it provided a permanent critique of prevailing religious beliefs, operating in available gaps, serving as both critique and confirmation. Jung regarded it as a projection of psychic processes onto matter, a metaphor for psychological growth and a continuation of Christian mysticism 'carried on in the subterranean darkness of the unconscious'.[11] The repeated phrase *solve et coagula* lay at the heart of the alchemic process, which remains obscure but can be simplified into three stages. First, *calcinatio, melanosis* or 'blackening', in which the adept underwent an apparent death as the *prima materia* was broken down. Second, *leukosis* or *albedo*, a 'whitening' in which the adept's identity was regained on a higher plane. Thirdly, *rubedo* or *iosis*, in which opposites were reconciled, a process which, in the manuals, was imaged by a sacred wedding between the adept in the guise of a (red, solar) King and the undifferentiated cosmos in the form of a (white, lunar) Queen. In alchemical texts this coupling was often illustrated as an act of incest perfomed in a bath of salt water. Laden with baptismal and lunar associations, salt, in Jung's phrase 'an arcane substance', was identified with Mercurius, the principal symbol of *prima materia* or the recipe to be worked on.[12] Black and foul-smelling to begin with, it is described by alchemists in terms of faeces and graves. And salt is a good choice; as Jung pointed out, it 'becomes impure and pure of itself, it dissolves and coagulates itself, or, as the sages say, locks and unlocks itself'.[13] It comes as no surprise that salt has been interpreted as a symbol of the entire alchemical process.

Regarded as a contribution to that argument about material form which underlay critical discussions about 'conceptualism', alchemy seems to augment the range of available modes, while meshing with ideas of structure as process which offered one route out of Minimalism. The main forerunner of this approach was undoubtedly Marcel Duchamp. (Hence the famous exchange with Robert Smithson in a New York gallery. 'I see you're into alchemy,' said Smithson, looking at the work. 'Yes,' Duchamp replied, and their only meeting was at an end.[14]) Throughout the 60s and 70s experts on Duchamp such as Arturo Schwarz, Maurizio Calvesi, Octavio Paz and Jack Burnham decided that the programme that underlay *The Large Glass* was indisputably alchemical.[15] Despite a disavowal on his part and the theory of Ulf Linde that every aspect of his alchemy was drawn from the same book, Albert Poisson's *Théories et symboles des alchimistes* (1891), general opinion changed accordingly.[16] When it was suspected, then proved, that while Duchamp had pretended to be in retirement he had instead been working on a secret installation, *étant donné: 1er la chute d'eau 2e le gaz d'éclairage*, the idea of an embattled, wilful obscurantist met no more serious challenges. The male and female aspect, the glass in which chemical changes were to happen, the androgynous poses of Duchamp himself in his disguise as Rrose Sélavy . . . These and many other pieces of evidence were presented at a time when Duchamp's influence had never been so powerful. Even his punning pseudonym came to seem less absurd: 'Marchand du Sel', or salt-seller.

As Duchamp's career showed, alchemy, *le grand oeuvre,* was a lifetime's occupation. Onwin's aesthetic, as presented in *The Recovery of Dissolved Substances,* made it clear that he agreed. As the book goes on and the range of reference extends further and further, so the references to privacy, loneliness and longterm application increase. Making such an appeal carries its own implications. Fernand Braudel theorised about a way of writing history which would transcend individuals and particular events; he saw man as a victim of climate, vegetation, kinds of agriculture and mental frameworks, and ends one of his books with these words: 'When I think of the individual I am always inclined to see him imprisoned in a destiny in which he has little hand, tied in a landscape in which the infinite perspectives of the long term stretch into distance both behind him and before.'[17] The absence of free choice, the brevity of a single existence, the unimportance of change, above all the total power of natural conditions over the individual as Braudel sees it in his theory of the *longue durée,* find an echo in Onwin's point of view as expressed in this early period of his career. Yet this was about to change. Among other things, the salt marsh was a metaphor for homeostasis, that integration which Jung

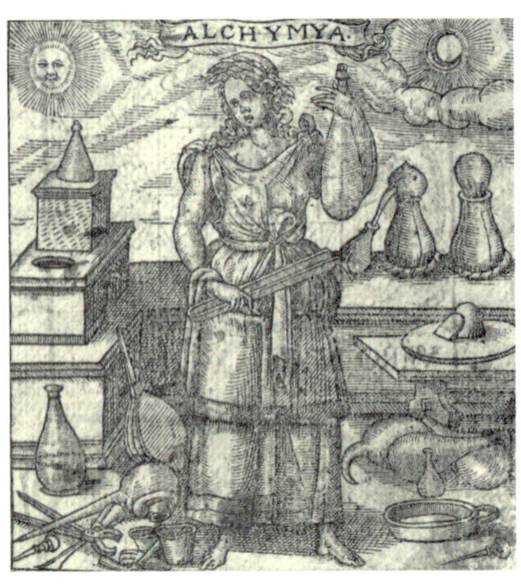

[2]

saw as the aim of psychoanalysis and which ecological theorists were beginning to propose restoring to earth. In 1979 James Lovelock published his book *Gaia: A New Look at Life on Earth,* which argued that the conditions needed for life on earth are maintained in a process of continual feedback — in other words, that under normal circumstances, the planet is self-regulating and maintains conditions suitable for existence. These are abnormal circumstances, however; as a living organism, it is forced to face unusual challenges, such as deforestation, the greenhouse effect and the pollution of the oceans. Gradually, it became clear that the salt marsh experience had its political aspect too, as did alchemy, for if the decline of alchemy ushered in modern science and the 'de-enchantment of the world', the onset of the idea that matter did not have a mind, then Green politics might reverse that state of affairs, 're-enchant' the world and persuade us of our duty to tend the mother-goddess, Gaia, the world as a sensate organism.[18] Perhaps a revolution in thought is necessary to bring about a state of affairs in which Braudel's eventless history could once more be written. 'Alchemy,' wrote Jung, 'is the herald of a still unconscious drive for maximal integration which seems to be reserved for a distant future.'[19] The future has moved nearer than he imagined. [2]

In 1988 Glen Onwin showed a set of works made over the previous five years, works which not only extended his previous considerations of the integration theme but also reflected the growing awareness of world crisis. The *Revenges of Nature* series elevated that 'drive for maximal integration' from the realm of the individual human psyche to that of our entire planet.

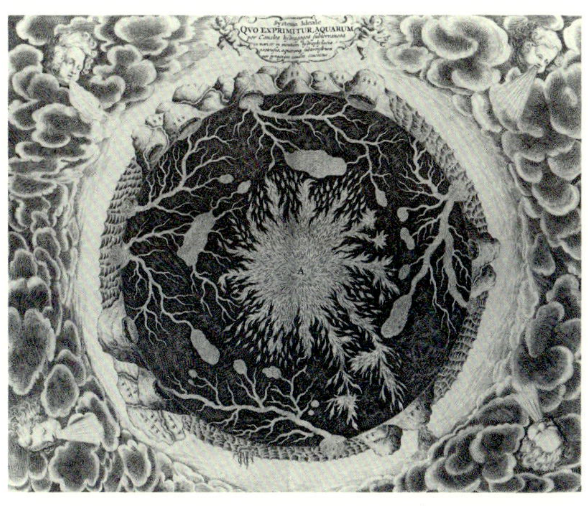

[3]

Instead of employing paint or what I have called 'allotropic' combinations of materials in these vast wall-pieces he used substances which actually *were* allotropic, like wax, ferns or sulphur, deliberately jumbling metaphorical and literal readings and breaking down the idea of a fictive realm which 'art' is frequently supposed to inhabit. If this Brechtian 'alienation effect' succeeded in emphasising that actual political issues were involved, it was counterbalanced by a high increment of symbolism; indeed, the titles of the works reflected the variation between alchemical and purely historical. *Massa Confusa, Peacock's Tail, Terra Damnata* and *Albedo* — respectively, the initial material, an effect of the light at one stage of the process, the scum which must be thrown away and the 'whitening' stage — take their place somewhere between the start of life on earth (*First Life*) and the prospect of its destruction (*Unthinkable*). Somehow the choice of materials for the paintings made them unexpectedly complicit. Whether they existed as a set of possibilities or a forlorn hope is unclear. And without the help of titles, total abstractions take on an alarming relativity of scale. The viewer could have been watching vast tongues of lava leaping from the surface of the sun or looking through a microscope at some equally violent sign of erupting energy. Borrowing from Athanasius Kircher, the seventeenth-century Jesuit polymath, who believed that rivers of water and fire ran through the earth from side to side [3], Onwin produced paintings that recalled both cosmology and microscopy, while drawing on a figure who might be regarded as a populariser.[20] And though in doing that Onwin was also opting for a larger audience, the permanent strangeness of the material, the wonder of organic matter which has played an increasingly large part in his work, was necessary for other than alchemical reasons. Recalling the times of 'primitive' science, when materials were imbued with the characteristics of people and gods, both Christian and pagan, as well as being shrouded by secret terminology, and where metaphors of life and death, destruction and fertilisation, preserved their potency, Onwin had always succeeded in conveying his own sense of interconnectedness, which (in formal and strategic terms) wistfully recalled the medieval convention of *correspondentia*, that Great Chain of Being which connected every level of the universe.[21] The single difference between this and the facts of late twentieth-century life is simply stated. While medieval man believed that his place and power were predetermined, his modern counterpart believes that change may be possible.

In *As Above So Below*, made for Square Chapel in Halifax, Onwin was offered an ideal site: an empty building in the form of a covered cube, with two floors. The first and major decision was to close the doors on the ground floor, and to use a temporary staircase in order to allow visitors to enter the upper floor first. Once inside, the bare roof joists and the ruined central ceiling rose, above all the four sets of five windows vied for attention. Onwin's single addition was a huge, low, square trough of black brine with wax floating on the surface. Between those islands of congealed wax, crystalline archipelagoes developed, more or less of them depending on the weather. Always visible in the water a few feet in front of the viewer, wherever the standpoint, the central ring of white plaster could be seen. Yet this and the wax and salt took second place to the reflection of the roof, even deeper, it seemed, than the ceiling was high, like a shipwreck in a clear pool, or a view to the floor below, seen from a high ledge. One thing was certain; the Narcissus effect had been rendered impossible; people could not exist in this reflected world. Before the altar in Winchester Cathedral stands a large, rectangular mirror, like the ones Victorian ladies used. Yet there is one difference: this one pivots in the middle and reflects the famous vaulted ceiling. Looking into the pool at Square Chapel conveyed something of the same effect: of an exactly symmetrical, equally unattainable view. Yet the differences outweighed the similarities. From the experience of the outside of the building and the memory of the height already climbed, visitors intuited an equal space below them. This, together with the inability to gauge the position and safety of the self — how frequently mirrors are used simply to provide reassurance, after all — disconcerted the viewer, just at the point where the descent was about to begin. The route, down a narrow flight of stairs, led to darkness. Lighting was subdued, and predominantly green, the ceiling was lower than expected and at first it looked like a dead end. Then a central corridor was located, with long, glass tubes at each end, one containing red liquid, the other green, each with a light of the same colour trained on it. To one side of this a two-part work extended, with two kinds of material — coal and gypsum, one organic and one inorganic — resting in troughs of white and black brine respectively. On the other side, first a mysterious, flat bed of bitumen was to be found and, on top of that, glass phials full of green organic juices and salt and copper sulphate solution on the tarry surface. In the farthest room, only visible from a single position in the central corridor, lay a glowing container with a thick, green coil sunk into the centre. Then the path led back down the dim corridor, to the right, and a second view of the double trough and rocks before ascending into the light upper storey and finally down the exterior steps to ground level.

To begin with, two experiences of verticality are offset: the reflection of the roof in the water and the fact that a real lower level exists, where night replaces day, dream for reality, and, because the entrance is on the second floor, below-ground for above. The idea that an underground lies below our own was a common feature of ancient cultures. The Greeks thought so, and the Egyptians even believed that in that world the dead walked upside-down, with the contents of their bowels dropping from their mouths. One critic suggested a parallel to Onwin's working-methods in the idea of the 'night sea journey'.[22] Instead, this installation reminds us of the *nekyia*, a harrowing of hell like Dante's, or that of Hercules who begins his mythic life as a strongman and ends as a Christ figure. Below, in the crypt, where darkness replaces light, lies a 'cryptic' subterranean world, a dream world with an inverse relation to daily life. Here raw, unrepressed materials lie closeted, like excreta. 'The day's residues,' Freud called dream matter. To look into the self and study the operations of dream meant going through Hell, he believed, with all the agony that implied. (The epigraph to his *Traumdeutung* was from Virgil's *Aeneid*: 'If I cannot bend the higher powers, I will move Acheron.' Similarly, Jung compared the resistance to delving too deeply into oneself as 'the fear of the journey to Hades.'[23]) If images of heroism occur with predictable regularity when talk turns to the analysis of dreams, the reason is not hard to find. The descent into this particular underworld means confronting loss and void, which has turned into its opposite: matter. Dead souls wander here, with messages to convey, and what, we have persuaded ourselves, is over and done with returns to be settled properly. What we thought was dead still walks. There is no escape.

One Greek word for the dead is *skia* or 'shade'. Engaging with such beings, one dream theorist has suggested, is as difficult as catching sight of one's own shadow, a perception of perception. 'So . . . entering the underworld is like entering the mode of reflection or mirroring . . . we may enter the underworld by means of reflection, by reflective means: pausing, pondering, change of pace, voice or glance, dropping levels.'[24] This description corresponds closely to the experience of walking downstairs at Square Chapel. Intent on ignoring references to growth and forgetting, in the form of the wax and crystals, by the time visitors reach the stairs they are still blinded by that first great reflection which suggests that no 'under' exists, nor indeed an 'over', since the impression of the former and the purely visual hint of the latter have united, or been matched almost perfectly, in the mirror-like surface of the murky water. 'As above, so below . . .'[25] Exchanging dream for reality, night for day, is possible only by means of a form of reflection. Indeed, the very building is founded on a confrontation with oneself, a perception of perception in a darkened place with dead ends, where even the idea of reaching a far point and being forced to double back is imbued with significance. As early as his discovery of the salt marsh, Onwin had been fascinated by the moment when the water stops rising and for a short time no activity is visible until it flows out again. Examining the cracked mud afterwards, he found the turn of the tide marked there. Go far enough with one movement and another will set in, Jung believed: '*Les extrêmes se touchent.*' He called this state *enantiodromia*. In the past, Onwin had connected it with a change of state or mind. Now, unexpectedly, it signified equivocation, a pause at the turning-point of a journey, when something is to be learned. But what? In that cave-like space, womb and tomb, disorientation becomes the norm. Yet one thing is clear; just as the upper floor thrives on the doubling of image, the crypt 'doubles' for what is above by announcing that below is where meaning is to be found. Here everything echoes our own equivocation, the feeling of having come this far and learned so little. The mass of raw ingredients resembles a fecund slime where the raw ingredients of life are to be found and, in time, may even emerge as life. But not yet. Opposite, the Oriental garden of marooned rocks conveys opposing, self-cancelling messages, linking gradual growth and change with decay, organic with inorganic life. Yet there is no apparent issue.

The glass tubes, red and green, signal STOP and GO at once, an exercise in cancellation. Even their title is equivocal: *Pharmacy*, after Marcel Duchamp.

Made in 1914, *Pharmacy* was what Duchamp called a 'rectified ready-made'. He found a greetings card of a winter landscape in a shop and, remembering red and green lights he had seen while looking into a railway tunnel, added spots of both colours. Were they meant to represent those familiar glass jars in the windows of chemists' shops? Or were they intended to be figures? Or both? As a wedding present for his sister Suzanne, Duchamp gave her the painting *Young Man and Girl in Spring*. On the occasion of her divorce from her husband he presented her with *Pharmacy*, as if it was something to be celebrated. Four years later, when she remarried, this time to Jean Crotti, a friend of Duchamp, he gave her his *Unhappy Readymade*, a book to be hung outside and left hanging. The alchemical references in *Young Man and Girl in Spring* were established by Arturo Schwarz in 1969, who commented on the element of 'unconscious incestuous love' which led Duchamp to send his sister so many coded messages in the form of artwork.[26] Each revealed much of his own state of mind — jealous of the nuptials, left out in the cold, ready to hang himself. (In another essay published eight years later, Schwarz took pains to emphasise the *unconscious* aspect of his affection.) It would not be fanciful to interpret *Pharmacy* as an updating of the wedding present. The naked figures leaping toward a common centre have gone. So has the sunlight and the blossom. It is winter. They stand side by side in a far cooler landscape making no attempt to communicate. Yet at the same time there is 'light at the end of the tunnel'. After all, a chemist's shop is a welcome sight in a snowbound landscape. Help is at hand, it may seem. Yet even this is in doubt. As Derrida has pointed out, in Greek, *pharmakon* or 'drug' can be translated as either 'cure' or 'poison'.

Occurring as a rider to an already overrich joke, the 'kill or cure' inference is characteristically Duchampian. (Even his one-line remark dissociating himself from alchemy is still being interpreted as if it were a fragment of Wittgenstein.[27])

At the pivotal point of Onwin's Halifax installation, *Pharmacy* suggests a zero point where an overload of meaning is shrugged off, a deflection of 'depth' which parallels the visual phenomenon upstairs. Read alongside the contents of the other rooms, it gains in significance, however. One of these has not yet been discussed. The luminous circle in the last part of the lower room marks the end of the journey, which has no end at all. It glows with significance, as if the very act of refusing conclusion generated energy. Its meaning relies heavily on what has already been observed. As a circle in a square, it assumes a combative aspect, despite the fact that, more sweetly, a circle persisted in the square tank above. And at the very point at which the walker must turn back, it makes an event of that turning, suggesting that an entire journey is needed in order to feel its significance.

As an alchemical and psychoanalytic symbol, it takes the form of the *uroboros* or dragon, representing the permanent dissolving, evaporating and distilling of matter involved in the alchemical process.[28] Bisexual, self-sufficient, this miraculous snake eats itself, spits itself out, kills itself and spawns itself over and over again [4]. With the androgyne, the progeny of the

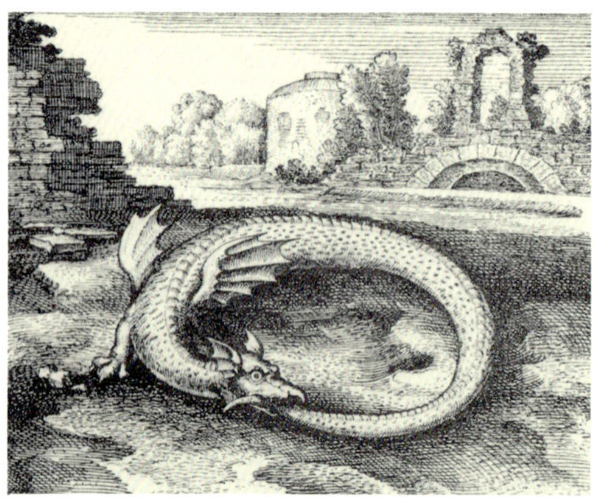

[4]

union of the King and Queen, sun and moon, it is a symbol of perfection, union and process.[29] Jungian theorists saw it as a symbol of the consciousness that prevailed in the womb, where inside and outside, the world and the unconscious, fused. A square reflection upstairs, confusing three different spaces — one three-dimensional, one a plane, one a mirage — and a circular tube downstairs, as closed as its counterpart is open, looking inside while the bath upstairs looked out; the confusion of decay and growth, the stagnant and the fecund, waste and vegetation; the square above, the circle below; the grotesque actuality of dream below, the seductive fragility of reality above . . . Onwin's play of modalities has never been so intricate, or so aligned with states of consciousness, faith and the grounds of faith. For this is a ruined chapel, after all, and visiting it becomes a kind of pilgrimage, an experience that traditionally combines religion with ritual journey.[30]

Separating him- or herself from society for a time, the pilgrim voluntarily enters a limbo where laws of daily existence are suspended and transition from one state or status to another can be effected. Traditional threshold rituals — waiting outside doors, being ushered in, turning back momentarily on leaving — are elaborated while concealment, mystery and darkness prevail. In this liminal state, the neophyte feels that birth and death are confronted simultaneously. Invisibility and bisexuality seem imminent. The entire experience could be regarded as a glimpse of a condition where definitions hold no sway. In this wilderness everyone is equal.

Starting out as an artist in a confused time, Onwin made that confusion his theme, and set out to grasp the meaning of materiality. For him, as for Italian *arte povera* practitioners, the answer lay in nature, life and death and problems of survival.[31] 'That which is above is like that which is below,' the Emerald Tablet instructs us, 'And as all things have been derived from one . . . so all things are born from this one thing.'[32] The statement takes the form of a circle. And, as the willing 'pilgrim' confronts the treasures in the vault, it seems that whereas the initial station of the journey was all evanescence and duplicity, the far point of that journey is zero, an empty cipher.[33]

Yet at this far point, in the dark centre of the building where the valueless and valuable are equalised, the foetal and the fecal are elided, where matter becomes *mater*, an Earth Mother,[34] the *uroboros* which symbolises the stirrings of consciousness and individual identity provides a cue for inspiration, revelation, a sounding of the godlike voices that were present and are now lost to us.[35] And, as if to rephrase the same point, the site itelf is permitted its full symbolic resonance. In mythical terms, the ruin should lead us to remember the destruction of Solomon's Temple in 586 BC, regarded as the breaking of a bond between heaven and earth.[36] Since that was a cosmic catastrophe, the rebuilding is regarded as a cosmic restoration, the celebration of a spiritual and personal bond between God and His people. And God *is* the Temple. ('Yet will I be to them as a little sanctuary' — *Ezekiel* 40.2.) If the upper floor recalls the direct links of the Christian God with His world, the half-darkened crypt speaks of the roots of the faith, not patriarchal but matriarchal, based not on spirit vs. flesh but on the properties of matter alone.

Enantiodromia as bathos, a turning back apparently empty-handed, having seen something without realising what has been seen . . . The vision of a reality as slim as a meniscus, resisting any reference to the viewer, as if the 'reflection' it offered were one on modality itself and nothing more, while the 'earthly' or hellish or dreamlike underworld becomes an allotropic museum . . . By the end of the journey, frustration has set in. The pilgrim feels left out, let down, abandoned. Yet isn't this just another phase of any liminal experience? Returning to society, the pilgrim feels that the problem has been stated more clearly, even though the answers remain mysterious. All that is needed is some deeper understanding of one's own inner workings and the kind of passion for synthesis that alchemists possessed. Does their passion, or a version of it, imply the symbolic rebuilding of the temple, a tangible token of God's covenant with mankind? Or is it an act of heresy to suppose that the base and the precious can change places, that a communion wafer really becomes Christ's body?

Obsessed with properties of matter, Onwin also dwells on changes of mind: that cusp between alchemy and modern scientific thought on which Newton was poised, or the necessary leap that may now propel scientists into a future where they regard the universe as a creative, self-regulating entity?[37] Leading directly from the saltmarsh experience, his art, like alchemy, resembles a lifetime's search for enlightenment, a deliberate confrontation with mysteries and a willingness to break rules. For even siting his present work in a place originally dedicated to orthodox worship resembles an act of rule-breaking. His approach — to cast the question back to the questioner — has Oriental parallels, no doubt.

In this particular work, in this particular place, Gnostic precedents seem more relevant. Gnosticism or 'secret knowledge' meant insight, some knowledge not of the God we imagine when the word 'God' is spoken, but of an underlying power of which our 'God' is merely an image. This knowledge is reached by insight into the self, not unlike that which psychotherapy now offers. Whoever gains the secret knowledge becomes 'no longer a Christian but a Christ', according to one of the Gnostic gospels.[38] The result of such a belief must have been subversive, to say the least. According to the Gospels of Matthew, Mark and Luke, Jesus proclaimed an imminent and literal Kingdom of God. In the Gnostic Gospels that 'Kingdom' symbolises transformed consciousness.

> Jesus saw infants being suckled. He said to His disciples, 'These infants being suckled are like those who shall enter the Kingdom.' They said to him, 'Shall we, then, as children, enter the Kingdom?' Jesus said to them, 'When you make the two one, and when you make the inside like the outside and the outside like the inside, and the above like the below, and when you make the male and the female one and the same . . . Then you will enter.'[39]

The comparison with the Emerald Tablet is striking. Like the Gnostics, Onwin takes our questions of art, existence and even faith and flings them back in our faces. Internal transformation, he implies, is the only key. Yet there is still a long way to go, a closer understanding of the literal and metaphorical, of what transformation does or could imply.

Stuart Morgan

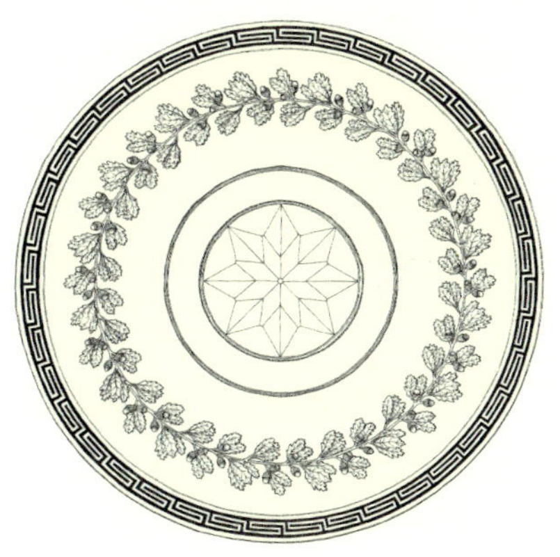

THE ARCHITECTURE OF THE SQUARE

In an attempt to identify the extent of religious non-conformity in the diocese of York Archbishop Herring's Visitation Returns for 1743 enquired amongst its ministers the number of dissenters within each parish and the location of their places of worship. Replies varied widely. The vicar of Moor Monkton reported with satisfaction: 'There are about sixty Families in my Parish; and Praised be God, never had any Dissenters among us of any kind whatever'. At Epperston there was 'no meeting house . . . blessed be God'. At Bradford there were 'Teachers called Methodists, who sometimes come amongst us, and draw great numbers after them, but the times and places of their Meetings are uncertain'.[1] Others confessed to hearing of secret assemblies in private houses or barns, and sometimes of public preaching in the open streets. Occasionally chapel buildings were mentioned: at Birstall there were three Presbyterian meeting houses and one each for Anabaptists and Quakers as well as twelve or thirteen unlicensed boxes. Halifax boasted three Quaker houses with congregations numbering some two hundred, and in 1743 a 'new one' was under construction.[2] Earlier, on her 'Great Journey to Newcastle' in 1698 Celia Fiennes had found Halifax 'almost ruined and come to decay', though she noted 'many good people and a large Meeting'.[3] Twenty-five years later, Daniel Defoe mentioned a dozen or so chapels-at-ease and some sixteen meeting houses in the town.[4] In fact, there was considerable non-conformist building activity in Yorkshire during the first half of the eighteenth century, though many of these so-called 'chapels' were no more than rooms in private houses, cottages and barns adapted for worship rather than purpose-built: small, makeshift, inadequate and unable to rival the aesthetic achievements of their Anglican neighbours. From the 1740s, however, the evangelising successes of Dissenting ministers like William Grimshaw of Howarth, John Wesley and George Whitefield resulted in more substantial and sophisticated designs, of which perhaps the most remarkable is Square Chapel, Halifax.[5]

The Revd Titus Knight (1719–93), instigator of Square Chapel, was a local collier who had converted to Methodism in his teens but withdrew from the sect on doctrinal grounds in 1762.[6] On 20 November of that year Revd Grimshaw wrote to Selina, Countess of Huntingdon that Knight was 'actively labouring to rescue sin-slaved souls from the kingdom of darkness . . . The people among whom he is sowing the seed of the kingdom are poor, their means are very limited, yet the Lord has put it in their hearts to build a house for the preaching of his word. Now I have come to the point — can your Ladyship spare a mite to aid these worthy souls?'[7] By 1763, having been ordained into the Congregational (or Independent) ministry as preacher of Chapel in Fold, Halifax, Knight was fulminating on sin and righteousness.[8] This chapel, consisting of two converted cottages laying between Woolshops and Goal Lane, soon proved far too small and so (according to the *Members' Book* compiled by Knight and his Vestry) 'with a longing desire to hear the word of God, and regarding Providence, a sense of duty put us upon making some attempt to gratify their [the congregation's] desire. But our present House not being capable of enlargement, we procured a convenient soil whereon to build a new one. The Bretheren ... fired with a laudable zeal for the cause of God and precious souls, have liberally contributed towards the expense, some of them far beyond what might have been expected'. This amounted to about £400, including Knight's contribution of 10 guineas. With other members of the congregation, he managed to gather £132 *2s 9d* during a fund-raising campaign which took them to Bridgnorth, Bristol, Kidderminster, Nantwich, Newport and Worcester; another £163 *12s 6d* came from well-wishers in Birmingham, Coventry, Warwick and Wolverhampton, while the Revd Henry Venn of Huddersfield collected £170 on a visit to London: in all £738 *2s 6d* during the period of construction, with an additional £102 *10s 0d* after the consecration of the new chapel, which is said to have cost a total of £2,000.[9]

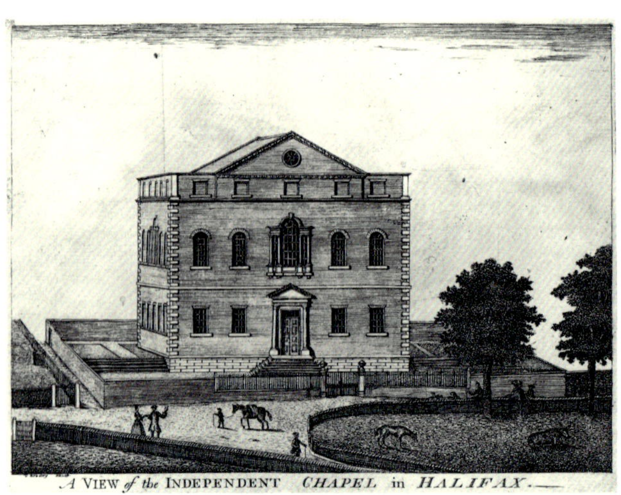

[1]

Because the identity of the architect is unknown and no contemporary drawings or building accounts can be found, the designing and construction history of Square Chapel remains shrouded in mystery. Work apparently began in 1771 and the New Chapel, as it was then called, opened on 24 May of the following year: the date 1772 at one time filled the central panel of the blind attic on the west front. The earliest recorded view [1], an engraving from the north-west published in Nelson's *The History of the Town and Parish of Halifax*, 1789, and signed 'T. Bradley DELIN' (for delineator), has given rise to the credible suggestion that the designer was the Halifax architect, Thomas Bradley (1753–1833).[10] Son of a local joiner of the same name, he would have been eighteen years old in 1771, fresh from his apprenticeship to the trade and quite capable of working in the conservative, slightly awkward classicism which is a distinguishing mark of the chapel. It may be relevant that James Kershaw, one of the vestrymen superintending the building programme, had a sister-in-law named Mrs Bradley.[11] But perhaps young Thomas was merely earning a living as a topographical illustrator.

It is equally possible that Titus Knight had a hand in the design, just as John Wesley had dictated the architectural character of his meeting houses,[12] and here we are favoured with a remarkable piece of contemporary evidence. In 1772, fast on the building's completion, Knight published a long, twelve-page poem entitled *Hhadash Hamishcan: or, The New Chapel, at Halifax, in Yorkshire*, of which he was almost certainly also the author,[13] and which offers vital clues to his own ideas regarding the chapel's meaning.

The Meaning of the Square

Though originally called the New or Independent Chapel (and only from the early nineteenth century the Square), its unmistakable cubic form must have been regarded as its most distinctive feature from the start: a single cube of 60 feet long by 60 feet wide by 60 feet from the bottom of the rusticated basement (revealed in the 1789 print but later covered over) to the peak of the pediment. Unencumbered by steeple or by projecting porch or chancel — the traditional raiments of both Anglican and Catholic church design[14] — the Square possesses a uniformity of composition in the shapes and arrangements of doors and windows even to the insistent repetition of a Venetian Window (itself a form composed of circle and rectangle) in the middle of each of the four elevations so that internally they mirror one another across the great single auditory space of the preaching box.

Though non-conformist chapels in the eighteenth century tended to be boxy and austere, the particular striving at Halifax for a universal, classical geometry was uncommon, and this was forcefully accentuated by the overall use of red brick (with stone relegated sparingly to accents and dressings) in a town which until that moment had been constructed almost exclusively of local millstone grit and was known for its stoniness.[15] This sudden and

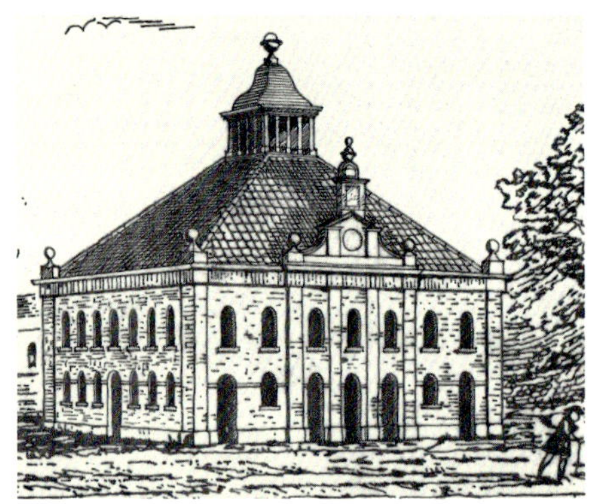

[2]

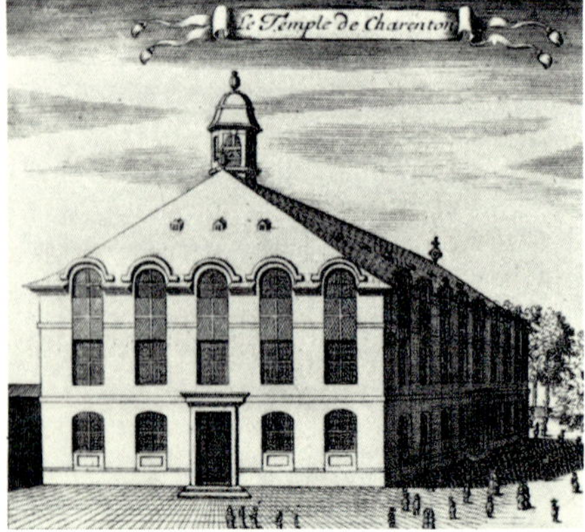

[3]

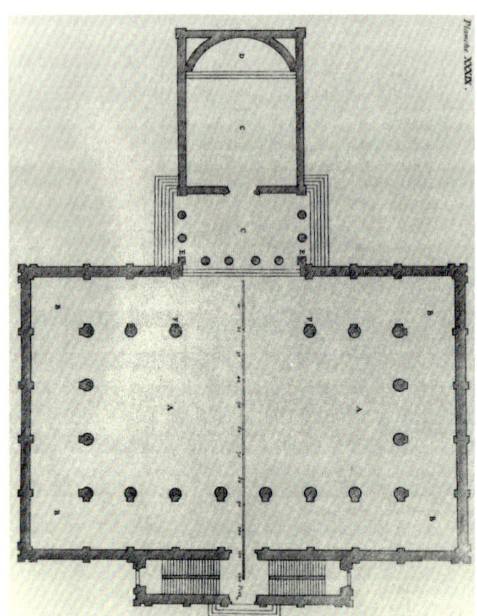

[4]

unexpected appearance of brick, therefore, may have been intended as a blatant confirmation of the increasing dissenter successes in the region.

But what is the precise meaning of the Square's *four-squareness*? In the 1760s Knight had regularly preached at George Whitefield's two celebrated London Tabernacles (or 'soul traps' as they were popularly called) located at Moorfields (built 1753) and in Tottenham Court Road.[16] The latter [2], built in 1756–60 as a large rectangle with uniformly round-headed windows and a lofty roof rising to a central cupola, was inspired by the most famous of all Protestant churches: the Calvinist Temple at Charenton near Paris [3], designed in 1623 by Salomon De Brosse and demolished by the mob soon after the Revocation of the Edict of Nantes in 1685. This building was in the form of a double cube (50 by 50 by 100 feet), with internal galleries supported on giant columns and a pulpit placed in the centre of the preaching space.[17] Such an unobstructed and capacious arrangement was subsequently recommended by the great English church architect, Sir Christopher Wren, so that Protestant congregations could 'hear distinctly, and see the Preacher', unlike in *'Romanist'* churches, where 'it is enough if they hear the Murmur of the Mass, and see the Elevation of the Host'.[18]

In turn, De Brosse modelled Charenton on Vitruvius's legendary Basilica at Fano in Italy (27 BC), which had already disappeared in Antiquity but

64

was the subject of various theoretical reconstructions [4] based on his own detailed description in *The Ten Books on Architecture*, which had appeared in many editions since its rediscovery in the Renaissance.[19] For us, the most significant feature of Fano, which Vitruvius described as possessing 'the greatest dignity and beauty', was that the main block measured 60 by 120 feet, that is, a double cube.

Vitruvius's exploration of universally harmonious forms in architecture, particularly the sphere and the cube, reflected his paramount concern for discovering an ideal system of proportions related to the human figure, graphically interpreted as 'homo ad circulum' | 'homo ad quadratum': a nude man with extended arms and legs circumscribed within a circle or square, and sometimes within both [5]:

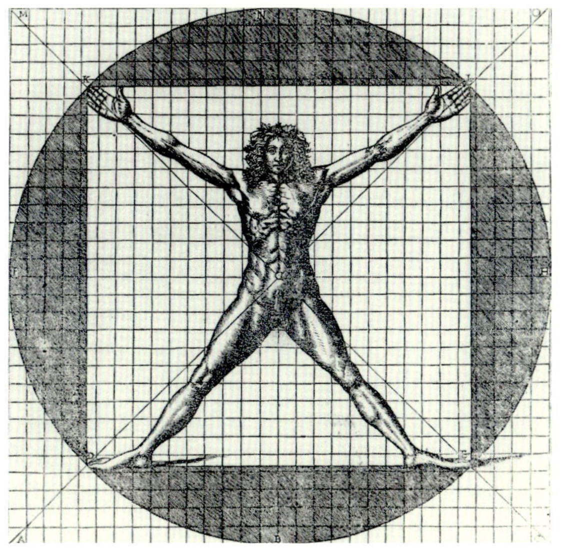

[5]

'First we shall talk of the proportions of man because from the human body derive all measures and their denominations and in it is to be found all and every ratio and proportion by which God reveals the innermost secrets of nature ... After having considered the right arrangement of the human body, the ancients proportioned all their work, particularly the temples, in accordance with it. For in the human body they found the two main figures without which it is impossible to achieve anything, namely the perfect circle ... and the square.'[20]

At Halifax [6], the pulpit, from where the minister preached the Word, was placed in the middle and towards the east wall, occupying the same position within the square as the head of Vitruvius's man.

Therefore, Vitruvius Man, Fano, Charenton (all patterns accessible to an enlightened eighteenth-century religious) and Tottenham Court Road (which Knight knew first-hand) suggest an inexorable path to Halifax. Knight himself offers a further and fascinating antecedent. The poem *Hhadash Hamishcan* (which incorporates the Hebrew word *mishkan*, tabernacle) opens with the questions:

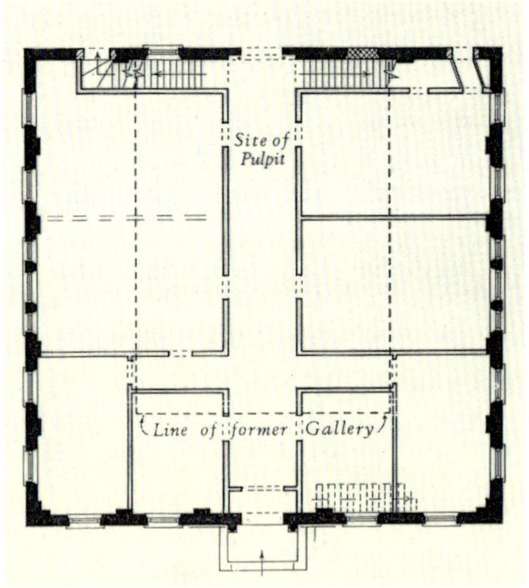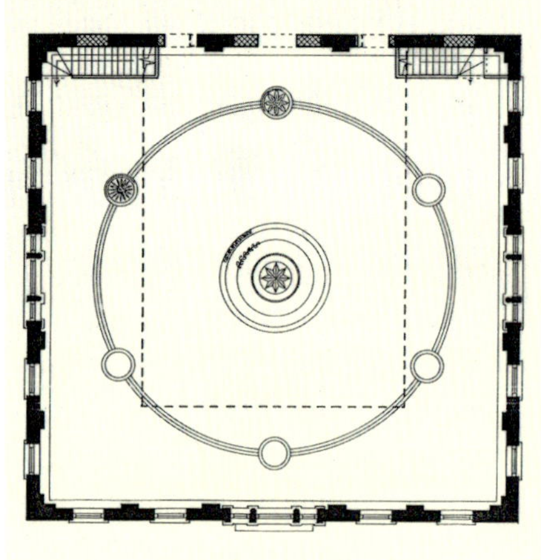

[6]

What is this Building, so magnificent,
With spacious Area, and this grand Ascent;
With Pillars on each Hand?

and answers:

One might suppose
The one was *Jachin*, and the other *Boaz*.
The Door-Steads built with architectal Grace,
Pilasters rising from the solid Base.

This is a reference to the famous twin columns flanking the entrance to Solomon's Temple at Jerusalem.[21] Further on, Square Chapel is directly compared to the sacred edifice:

But since you deem this House too large, and fine,
I'll lead your envious Thoughts to Palestine.
View foolish *Solomon*, at vast Expence,
Erect a House, which for Magnificence,
For Elegance, and Ornament, as far
Excell'd this House, as doth the Sun, a Star.
Yet the great Monarch of the Skies approv'd,

66

The Building, and the Gates of Zion lov'd.
Did Israel's favour'd Tribes (think you) transgress,
In off'ring freely in the Wilderness,
To build the Tabernacle God enjoin'd,
When each One brought the best of ev'ry Kind?[22]

The Old Testament description of the inner sanctuary of the Temple, the Holy of Holies wherein dwelt the Ark of the Covenant, gives its dimensions as 'twenty cubits in length, and twenty cubits in breadth, and twenty cubits in the height' (I Kings 6:19–20), that is, a cube of thirty by thirty by thirty feet which if multiplied eight times would be the equivalent volume of Square Chapel [7]. The Temple is the subject of a considerable European post-medieval literature which includes various attempts to reconstruct the appearance of the long-lost building. The most widely-known of these — J. B. Villalpando and H. Prado's *In Ezechielem Explanationes*, Rome, 1596–1605 and Bernard Lamy's *De Tabernaculo Foederis de Sancta Civitate Jerusalem et de Temple Ejus*, Paris, 1720[23] — show the sanctuary's exterior walls articulated with a regular rhythm of pilasters between

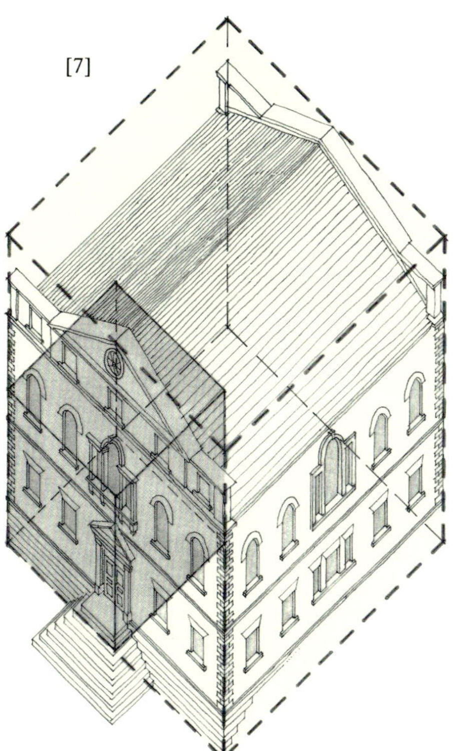

[7]

rectangular windows, an arrangement also favoured for the interior of Square Chapel [8]. In the latter, the capitals — composed of a series of vertical flutes rising from acanthus leaves [9] — are based closely on those in the peristyle of the Temple of Aesculapius, another celebrated ancient building, as engraved in Robert Adam's *Ruins of the Palace of the Emperor Diocletian at Spalatro*, 1764 [10].[24]

If these models seem to us much too sophisticated to be associated with the simple aspirations of a provincial dissenting congregation, it is worth remembering that in the eighteenth century the idea of the Jerusalem Temple appealed to a wide audience.[25] Moreover, it had entered into the repertory of Freemasonry iconography and, therefore,

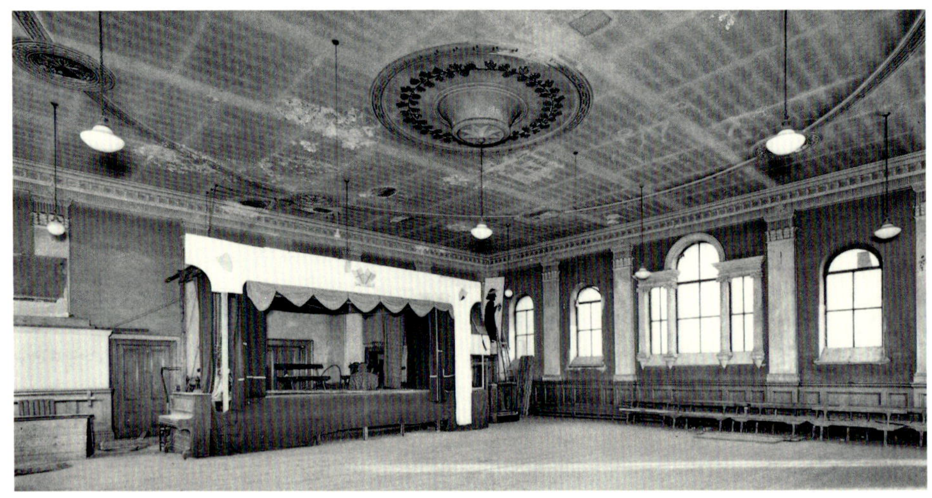

[8]

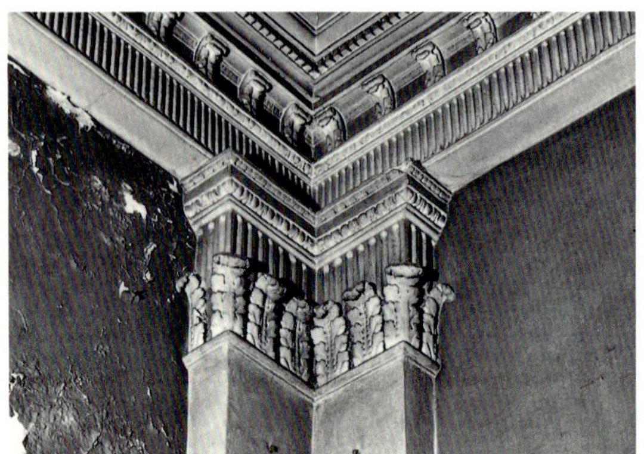

[9]

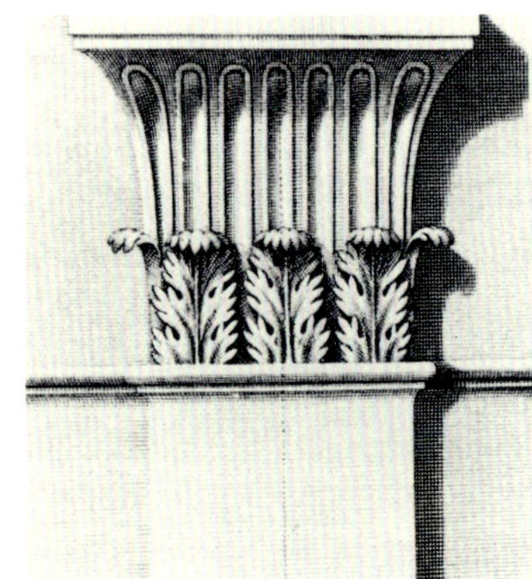

[10]

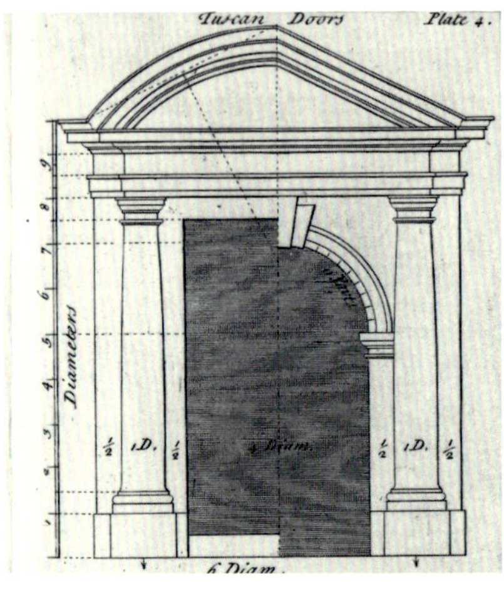

Tuscan Doors
Plate 4.
Diameters
½ 1D. ½
4 Diam.
½ 1D. ½
6 Diam.
[11]

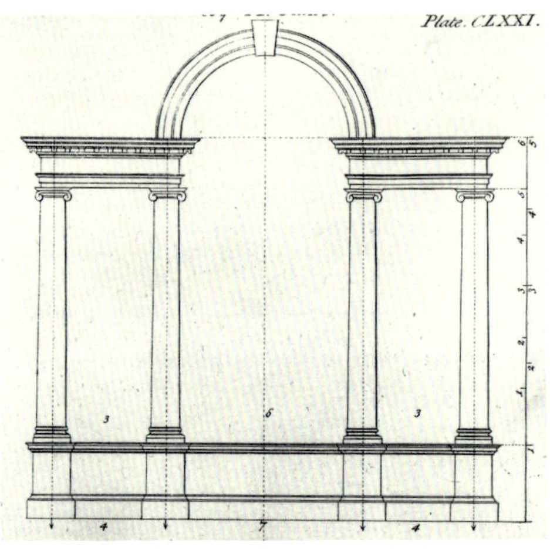

Plate. CLXXI.
3
6
3
4
7
4
[12]

was quite naturally closely associated with the building trades.

Batty Langley's *The Builder's Jewel: or, The Youth's Instructor, and Workman's Remembrancer*, published as an inexpensive pocket-book first in 1741 and thereafter in many editions (including three in 1768 and another in 1769), carries a masonic frontispiece [13] with plaques inscribed with the circle and cube, and a plan of a Freemasonry Lodge where the twin columns of Jachin and Boaz stand guardian.[26] Plate 4 [11] provided the pattern for the west door of Square Chapel. In turn, the Venetian Windows derive from Langley's *Ancient Masonry*, 1736 [12], a vast compendium of classical architectural patterns dedicated to the

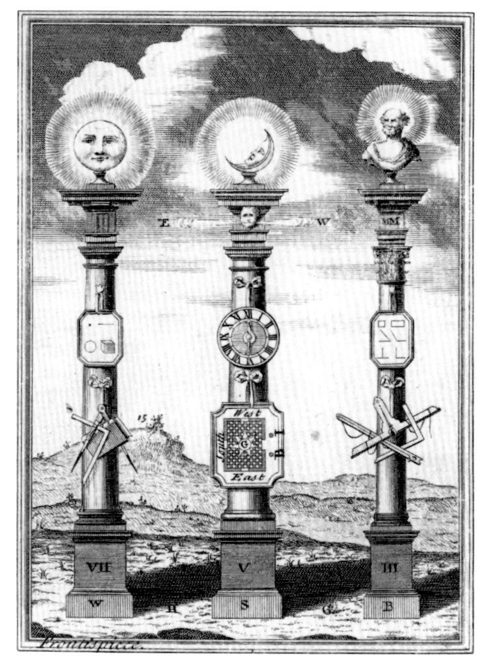

[13]

freemasonry fraternity, of which the author was a devout member.[27] Langley also wrote (in *The Grub-street Journal*) under the pseudonym Hiram, the builder of Solomon's Temple, and even named two of his sons Hiram and Vitruvius![28]

Titus Knight had published *Hhadash Hamishcan* in an attempt to repudiate the claims of critics that he had lavished 'vast Expence [and] Large Sums, in Ornaments [on] all this 'Waste'. While the exterior of the chapel subscribes to what the poet-vicar, William Mason on another occasion called 'plain Yorkshire taste',[29] it was suggested that the interior, with its richly-carved pulpit, pilasters, wainscot panelling and plasterwork (including a ceiling composed of key-pattern, acorns and leaves, which Knight described as 'flow'ry Work, of purest Paste',[30] alas, now almost entirely vanished), was certainly more magnificent than many non-conformist chapels of the day. Knight's critics, so he tells us in the poem, saw the Square as 'a Pantheon of the present Age', an explicit reference to James Wyatt's newly-opened, neoclassical pleasure dome, the Pantheon in Oxford Street, London (1769–72):

Have you the Building seen in Oxford-Road?
Profanely dedicated to ev'ry god.

Who of you, pleas'd, do not admire the Domes,
Superb, and lofty, and the spacious Room?[31]

Turning to the Halifax chapel:

But why such Beauty and Magnificence?
You might have built, and sav'd a vast Expence?
A House sufficient; but you here expend
Large Sums, in Ornaments, and to no End.

'Why all this Waste? 'Tis needless, serves no End.'
but Self to please, what will you not expend?[32]

The poem goes on for some pages in this vein.

This was a serious problem in a society which utterly rejected the 'Pageantry, and unnecessary Ornaments' associated with Papist churches.[33] So, Knight replied:

Forbear your Taunts, this Structure is design'd
An Habitation for th' eternal Mind.
Here, God the Saviour is to be ador'd

Here, heav'nly saving Truths are to be taught

The King of Glory is expected here

He cited, as we have seem, Solomon's Temple as a luxurious building dedicated to God, and asked:

Was that too elegant? Where ev'ry Pin,
Was in the Pattern giv'n, and Nothing mean?
Not *Oak*, but *Cedar*, *Shittim-Wood*, for *Fir*

Not *Iron*, but *Silver*, *Gold*, instead of *Brass*

And is it true, that God immensely great,
Will stoop to dwell with Men, in this low State?
What House can we, so elegant, and great,

As to be worthy of this Monarch's Feet?
Yet humbly trusting in thy faithful Word,
We dedicate this *House* to thee, O Lord

And in this House, which we have built for thee,
Set up thy throne, accompany thy word,
Let sinners hear, and fear, and seek the Lord.[34]

Knight envisaged 'all Things finish'd in a superb Taste',[35] and when Wesley visited the building soon after its completion he too found it 'finished with the utmost elegance'.[36] Though possessing nothing of the Glorious Gothic of the second Square Chapel (Joseph James, 1855–7, its ruins hovering nearby), Knight's building is also a far cry from Dean Swift's characterisation of Dissenters, in *A Tale of a Tub*, 1704, as those who *'feared* no Colours, but mortally *hated* all, and, upon that Account, bore a cruel Aversion to Painters', and who *'quarrel at the most innocent Decent Ornaments, and deface the Statues and Paintings on all the Churches in England.'*[37]

Terry Friedman

LIST OF ILLUSTRATIONS
AND REFERENCES

Illustration numbers given in square brackets [ ]

PERPETUAL POSSIBILITY   pp. 8–14

[1]   Electron microscope image of a hopper crystal of salt,
from *The Recovery of Dissolved Substances*, 1978
Photo University of Edinburgh

[2]   Salt-marsh, from *Saltmarsh*, 1974
Photo Glen Onwin

[3]   Detail of The Salt Room, from *The Recovery of Dissolved Substances*, 1978
Photo Eileen Lawrence

[4]   Glen Onwin, *Vortex of Degradation*, 1986.
Earth, organic matter, ash, metal, oil and wax on board, 244 × 264 cm
Photo Duncan McQueen

[5]   Glen Onwin, *Of Nature's Obvious Laws and Processes in Vegetation*, 1990.
Cupric sulphate, Sodium chloride, organic matter and wax. Installation in the under-
croft of the Bishop's Palace, Lincoln
Photo Heather Lees

THE ABOVE LIKE THE BELOW   pp. 45–58

[1]   Robert Smithson, *Spiral Jetty*, Great Salt Lake, Utah, 1970
Black rock, salt crystals, earth and water
Photo Gianfranco Gorgoni. Dwan Gallery, New York

[2]   'Alchymya', frontispiece from Conrad Gesner, *The Newe Jewell of Health*, tr. G. Baker,
London 1576
Photo by permission of The British Library

[3]   'Subterranean Water', from Athanasius Kircher, *Mundus Subterraneus*, Amsterdam 1665
Photo by permission of The National Library of Scotland

[4]   'The Dragon devouring his tail', Epigramma XIV, *Atalanta Fugiens hoc est Emblemata Nova de Secretis Naturae Chymica*, Michael Maierus, Frankfurt 1618
Photo by permission of The British Library

1. Lucy Lippard, *Six years: The Dematerialization of the Art Object*, London 1974.

2. Hal Foster, 'The Crux of Minimalism', in H. Singerman (ed.), *Individuals*, New York 1986, pp. 162–93.

3. C. Kuoni (ed.), *Energy Plan for the Western Man*, New York 1990, pp. 261–5.

4. Benjamin Buchloh, 'The Twilight of the Idol', *Artforum*, XIX, 1980, pp. 35 ff.

5. Keith Hartley, untitled essay in a pamphlet accompanying *Earth Icons: The Chymical Garden*, Bath 1988, n. p.

6. Glen Onwin, *The Recovery of Dissolved Substances*, Arnolfini, Bristol 1978.

7. Cf. Geoffrey H. Hartman, *Wordsworth's Poetry 1787–1814*, New Haven and London, p. 123.

8. James Lovelock, *The Age of Gaia*, Oxford 1988, p. 106.

9. E. Neumann, *The Origins and History of Consciousness*, Princeton 1970, p. 286.

10. Ibid., p. 287.

11. C. G. Jung, *Psychology and Alchemy* (*Collected Works*, tr. R. F. C. Hull, vol. 12), p. 245.

12. C. G. Jung, *Mysterium Coniunctionis* (*Collected Works*, tr. R. F. C. Hull, vol. 13), p. 189.

13. Ibid., p. 190.

14. N. Holt (ed.), *The Writings of Robert Smithson*, New York 1979, p. 198.

15. Arturo Schwarz, 'Duchamp et l'alchimie', in *Marcel Duchamp: L'Oeuvre*, Paris 1977; Arturo Schwarz, 'The Alchemist Stripped Bare in the Bachelor, Even', in *Marcel Duchamp*, ed. A. d'Harnoncourt & K. McShine, MoMA New York, and Philadelphia Museum of Art 1973; Maurizio Calvesi, *Duchamp Invisible*, Rome 1975; Octavio Paz, *Marcel Duchamp: The Castle of Purity*, London 1970; Jack Burnham, *Great Western Salt Works*, New York 1974, pp. 71–117.

16. Ulf Linde, 'L'ésoterique', in *Marcel Duchamp: L'Oeuvre*, Paris 1977, pp. 60–85.

17. Fernand Braudel, *The Mediterranean and the Mediterranean World in the Age of Philip II*, tr. S. Reynolds, London 1972–3, vol. 2, p. 1244.

18. Morris Berman, *The Re-Enchantment of the World*, Cornell 1981, *passim*.

19. C. G. Jung, *Mysterium Coniunctionis* (*Collected Works*, tr. R. F. C. Hull, vol. 30), p. 188.

20. Joscelyn Godwin, *Athanasius Kircher*, London 1979; James Birrell, 'The Failure of Excess', in *Revenges of Nature: Glen Onwin*, Fruitmarket, Edinburgh 1988, pp. 7–9.

21. A. O. Lovejoy, *The Great Chain of Being*, Cambridge Mass. 1936; E. M. W. Tillyard, *The Elizabethan World Picture*, Harmondsworth 1963.

22. Sandy Nairne, 'Voyage Nocturne en Mer', in *Un Certain Art Anglais*, Paris 1979, p. 109.

23. C. G. Jung, *Psychology and Alchemy* (*Collected Works*, tr. R. F. C. Hull, vol. 12), p. 439.

24. James Hillman, *The Dream and the Underworld*, New York 1979, p. 16.

25. Commonly used in alchemy, this phrase or some equivalent of it seems to turn up first in the 'Emerald Tablet' or *Tabula Smaragdina* of Hermes Trismegistos, a Hermetic document of pre-Islamic origin. 'Whatever is below is like that which is above, and whatever is above is like that which is below, to accomplish the miracles of the one thing', Titus Burckhardt, *Alchemy*, tr. N. Stoddart, Shaftsbury 1989, p. 196.

26. Arturo Schwarz, *The Complete Works of Marcel Duchamp*, London 1969, p. 98.

27. For a translation of Calvesi's interpretation of Duchamp's admission that he practised alchemy *'sans le savoir'* see John F. Moffitt, 'Marcel Duchamp: Alchemist of the Avant Garde', in M. Tuchman & J. Freeman (eds), *The Spiritual in Art: Abstract Painting 1890–1985*, Los Angeles / New York 1986, pp. 269 and 271.

28. E. Neumann, *The Origins and History of Consciousness*, tr. R. F. C. Hull, Princeton 1954, pp. 5–38 and *passim*.

29. E. Zolla, *The Androgyne*, 1981; A. J. L. Busst, 'The Image of the Androgyne in the Nineteenth Century', in I. Fletcher (ed.), *Romantic Mythologies*, London 1987, pp. 1–97; U. Prinz, *Androgyn: Sehnsucht nach Vollkommenheit*, Berlin 1986; Robert Knott, 'The Myth of the Androgyne', *Artforum*, November 1975, pp. 38 ff.; M. Eliade, *The Two and the One*, London 1965.

30. Drawing on A. van Gennep (*Rites of Passage*, tr. M. B. Vizedom & G. L. Caffee, 1977), Victor Turner refined and extended his terms. My account in this essay conflates van Gennep and Turner, drawing especially on Turner's *Image and Pilgrimage in Christian Culture* (with E. Turner), 1978, pp. 8, 231, 249; *Process, Performance and Pilgrimage*, New Delhi 1979, pp. 95, 121, 149, 153–5, 252; *The Drums of Affliction*, London 1981, pp. 269–70.

31. G. Celant, *Arte Povera*, New York 1969, p. 5. ('The artist-alchemist organizes living and vegetable matter into magic things, working to discover the root of things.')

32. This translation is quoted from Frances A. Yates, *Giordano Bruno and the Hermetic Tradition*, 1964.

33. Cf. F. A. Yates, *The Rosicrucian Enlightenment*, London 1975, p. 74. Quoting the *Fama Fraternitas*, she describes the subterranean vault 'lighted by an inner sun' as a central feature of the Rosencreutz legend.

34. P. Berry, 'What's the Matter with Mother?'. Lecture 190, London: Guild of Pastoral Psychology, 1978.

35. Julian Jaynes, *The Origin of Consciousness in the Breakdown of the Bicameral Mind*, New York 1976.

36. Henri Corbin, *Temple and Contemplation*, tr. P. Sherrard, London 1986.

37. B. J. T. Dobbs, *The Foundations of Newton's Alchemy*, New York 1975.

38. Elaine Pagels, *The Gnostic Gospels*, London 1979, p. 134, quoting the *Gospel of Philip* 67.26–7.

39. Ibid., p. 129; *Gospel of Thomas* 37.20–35.

THE ARCHITECTURE OF THE SQUARE pp. 61–71

[1]   Square Chapel, from Nelson, *The History of the Town and Parish of Halifax*, 1789

[2]   Whitefield's Tabernacle, 1756–60, Tottenham Court Road, London, from H. Phillips, *Mid-Georgian London*, 1964, fig. 304

[3]   Salomon De Brosse, Temple at Charenton, France, 1623 (anonymous engraving)

[4]   Vitruvius, Basilica at Fano, Italy, 27 BC, reconstruction of plan from Claude Perrault, *Les Dix Livres D'Architecture De Vitruve*, 1684, Livre V, Chapter 1, p. 152, pl. XXXIX

[5]   Vitruvius Man, from Cesare Di Lorenzo Cesariano's 1521 Como edition of Vitruvius, *De Architectura*

[6]   Square Chapel, plans of ground floor and gallery with ceiling decoration
Allen Tod Architects

[7]   The Holy of Holies of Solomon's Temple at Jerusalem (shaded cube) compared to Square Chapel
Allen Tod Architects

[8]   Square Chapel, interior of remodelled gallery level in 1970
Photo Royal Commission on the Historical Monuments of England

[9]   Square Chapel, detail of capital in 1970
Photo Royal Commission on the Historical Monuments of England

[10]   Capital of the Temple of Aesculapius, from R. Adam, *Ruins of the Palace of the Emperor Diocletian at Spalatro*, 1764

[11]   'Tuscan Doors', from B. Langley, *The Builder's Jewel*, 1741, Pl. 4
          Photo by permission of The British Library

[12]   'Venetian Window', from B. Langley, *Ancient Masonry*, 1736, Pl. CLXXI
          Photo by permission of The British Library

[13]   Frontispiece from B. Langley, *The Builder's Jewel*, 1741

1. S. L. Ollard and P. C. Walker, 'Archbishop Herring's Visitation Returns, 1743', *The Yorkshire Archaeological Society Record Series*, 1928–9, vol. LXXII (II) p. 174; LXXVII (IV) p. 49; LXXI (I) p. 59.

2. *Ollard*, I, p. 60; II, p. 32.

3. C. Morris, ed, *The Journeys of Celia Fiennes*, 1947, p. 221.

4. *A Tour Through the Whole Island of Great Britain*, 1724–6 (Everyman's Library edition, 1962, II, p. 198).

5. G. Hague, *The Unitarian Heritage: An Architectural Survey of Chapels and Churches in the Unitarian Tradition in the British Isles*, 1986, Chapters 2–3. D. Linstrum, *West Yorkshire Architects and Architecture*, 1978, pp. 194–9, pls. 154–5. C. F. Stell, *Calderdale Chapels*, Halifax Antiquarian Society, 1985, pp. 16–35.

6. J. Crabtree, *A Concise History of the Parish and Vicarage of Halifax*, 1836, p. 271. J. Watson, *The History and Antiquities of the Parish of Halifax*, 1775, p. 483. E. Winpenny, 'The Zeal of a Collier', *Halifax Evening Courier*, 6 October 1979.

7. Quoted in C. E. Seager, *Square Chapel and Church, Halifax*, undated typescript (courtesy Allen Tod Architects, Leeds).

8. *A Treatise on the Imputation of Sin, and of Righteousness*, 16 May 1766 (Yorkshire Archaeological Society, Leeds: Sermons 129F1).

9. Calderdale District Archives, Halifax: SC3 ('*Square Chapel Church Members' Book*'). 'The Sums subscrib'd, you honestly have paid; | But such as have with held their promis'd Aid, | I warn them — Be ye horribly afraid. | 'Tis Sacrilege, 'tis more than common Fraud, | The Injury's less done to Man, than God' (*Hhadash Hamishcan*, 1772, p. ll). The property is described in an indenture of 1773 as 'a parcel of Land . . . in the South East Corner of . . . Talbot Croft . . . adjoining to the new Square . . . 50 Yards [by] 57 yards . . . on which . . . a new Chapel hath been lately erected . . . adjoining . . . to the Road called Blackledge and also to the new Road leading from the Church Lane into the Square' (Calderdale District Archives, Halifax: RP 358 f. 6).

10. H. Colvin, *A Biographical Dictionary of British Architects 1660–1840*, 1978, p. 132. P. Smithies, *The Architecture of the Halifax Piece Hall 1775–1779*, 1988, pp. 15–20, pls 10–13.

11. E. Winpenny, 'Growing pains', *Halifax Evening Courier*, 13 October 1979.

12. *Linstrum*, p. 197.

13. On the title-page: 'Sold by T. Knight, Halifax. Price 2d . . . Printed by E. Jacob, for the Author . . . The Author doubts not, by his Name you'll guess, As Men are known to Men by Face, and Dress' (Yorkshire Archaeological Society, Leeds: 5A9). I am grateful for the assistance of Susan Leadbeater, the Society's Librarian.

14. 'The lofty Domes that most superbly rise, | The cloud-topp'd Tow'rs that seem to touch the Skies | Are low, and mean, and despicable, in his [God's] Eyes' (*Hhadash Hamishcan*, p. 12).

15. Celia Fiennes found Halifax 'a stony town' in 1698 (*Morris*, p. 221).

16. Moorfields Tabernacle, later demolished, is preserved in an engraving in the Museum of London. Tottenham Court Road Tabernacle, designed by Matthew Pearce, rebuilt 1892 (*Colvin*, p. 629).

17. Though utterly demolished as a result of the Revocation, which suppressed French

Protestant rights, the Temple was early immortalised in prints (R. Coope, *Salomon De Brosse and the Development of the Classical Style in French Architecture from 1565 to 1630*, 1972, pp. 183–7, pls 214–16).

18. 'The Letter of Sir Chr. Wren Upon the Building of National Churches', 1712 (*Wren Society*, IX, p. 17 item 6).

19. Book V, Chapter 1 (A. K. Placzek, ed., *Macmillan Encyclopedia of Architects*, 1982, vol. 4, p. 337). The first English edition, abridged, was published in 1692 and *The Architecture of M. Vitruvius Pollio: Translated . . . By W. Newton*, in 1771 (E. Harris, *British Architectural Books and Writers 1556–1785*, 1990, pp. 462–6).

20. Luca Pacioli, *De Divina Proportione*, quoted in R. Wittkower, *Architectural Principles in the Age of Humanism*, 1988, p. 25; also pls 6–11.

21. Page 3, with the note: '*Jachin*, signifies, he will establish — *Boaz*, there is strength in it, that is, the Lord will be the Strength, and a Pillar of Support unto his People'. In the eighteenth century these columns were thought to have been cast in metal and hollow; therefore, are they reflected in the Square Chapel in the enigmatic and structurally unnecessary pair of cast-iron columns embedded (and until recently unseen) in the internal west wall on either side of the main door?

22. Page 8.

23. H. Rosenau, *Vision of the Temple: The Image of the Temple of Jerusalem in Judaism and Christianity*, 1979, pp. 94–8, pls 96–100, 110–3. For an interesting discussion on the impact of these books on English architectural thought, see *Harris*, pp. 480–5.

24. G. Beard, *The Work of Robert Adam*, 1978, pl. 164.

25. *Rosenau*, p. 97, pls 109, 145–7, for Sir Isaac Newton's *Chronology of Ancient Kingdoms Amended*, 1728, and the Bath architect, John Wood's *The Origin of Building*, 1741; J. Rykwert, *The First Moderns: The Architects of the Eighteenth Century*, 1980, pp. 156–9 ill., for Revd William Stukeley of Spalding, Lincolnshire.

26. E. Beha, *A Comprehensive Dictionary of Freemasonry*, 1962, p. 39; J. Macpherson, 'Jachin and Boaz and the Freemasons' in B. F. Scholz, M. Bath and D. Weston, eds, *The European Emblem: Selected Papers from the Glasgow Conference*, 1990, pp. 129–51. See also J. S. Curl, *The Art and Architecture of Freemasonry*, 1991.

27. The west doors and windows of Westgate Unitarian Chapel, Wakefield, 1751–2 (see note 5) were lifted from pls XXXV, XL, LII in Langley's *The City and Country Builder's and Workman's Treasury of Designs*, 1750.

28. *Harris*, pp. 262–80.

29. He wrote to Horace Walpole, 9 August 1774: 'my curate and I are neither of us the dupes of fashion, but speak what we think in all simplicity. Treat us therefore with something more to *our* goût, and the world, even the great world, will not disdain to follow our plain Yorkshire taste' (W. S. Lewis, ed., *Yale Edition of Horace Walpole's Correspondence*, vol. 28, p. 165).

30. Page 3.

31. Pages 3 and 7, with the note: 'This Building is called the *Pantheon*, i.e. all the gods, meaning . . . that it is intended for every Kind of Sin'.

32. Page 4.

33. Jonathan Swift, *A Tale of a Tub. Written for the Universal Improvement of Mankind*, 1704 (11th edition, 1747, p. 140).

34. Pages 3, 8–10 respectively.

35. Page 3.

36. Quoted in *Stell*, p. 23. 'The building is very commodious . . . and its structure rather superb, the whole being finished in an elegant taste' (Nelson, *The History of the Town and Parish of Halifax*, 1789, p. 648).

37. See note 33 above.

AS ABOVE SO BELOW

Details of Installation

NIGREDO

Rendered brick tank, black dyed brine, wax and salt crystals

11.32 × 11.32 m × 25 cm

Room 18.13 × 18.27 × 8.93 m

PHARMACY

Glass tubes, red and green dyed water with vegetal tincture, with red and green lights

Each tube 2.45 m × 7.50 cm diameter

Corridor 2.70 × 13.10 × 3.78 m

ITS NURSE IS THE EARTH

The floor: Bitumen, copper sulphate solution, glass vials of vegetal extract and aluminium on a wood support with green light

6.12 × 4.62 m × 7 cm

The walls: Random configuration of 110 plates of various metals, 105 engraved with the symbols of the elements

Each plate 13 × 13 cm

Room 7.50 × 5.67 × 3.78 m

THE ONE TO THE ONE

Rendered brick tanks, black and white dyed brine, gypsum and coal with green light

9.70 × 4.98 m × 25 cm

Room 12.18 × 7.52 × 3.78 m

UROBOROS

Aluminium tank, brine, plastic tube and green dye with green light

3 × 3 m × 20 cm

Room 7.50 × 6.25 × 3.78 m

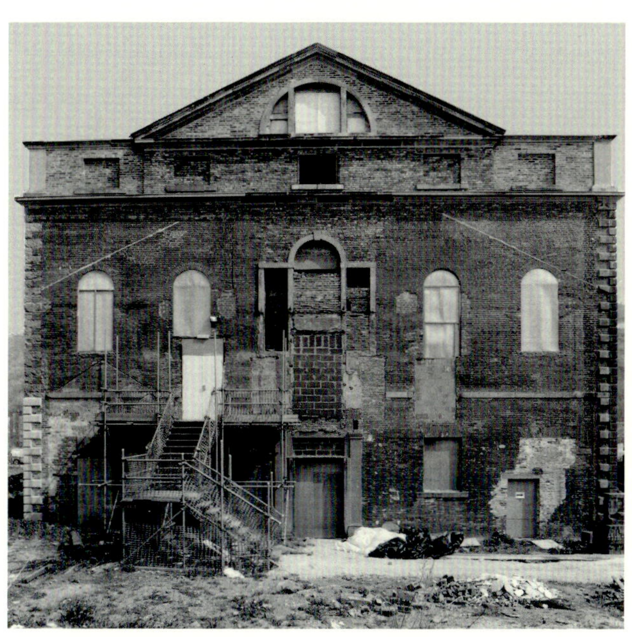

First published 1991
© The Henry Moore Sculpture Trust
and the authors

ISBN 0 9517783 0 7

Typeset in Plantin
1,250 copies printed on
Ikonorex Special Matt New Ivory
August 1991

Book design and production
Peter McGrath, Groundwork, Skipton

Reproduction and printing
Leeds Photo Litho
and Jackson Wilson, Leeds